DATE DUE

MAR 01 '94			

A PECULIAR MUSIC

Overleaf: A page from the notebook headed 'Emily Jane Brontë. Transcribed February 1844. Gondal Poems', probably the MS. 'discovered' by Charlotte in the autumn of 1845, preserved by the Rev. Arthur B. Nicholls long after the death of Emily and his wife Charlotte, and now in the British Museum. The first verse of this poem is quoted on p. 29.

——————— a A, M

O

Come, walk with me,
There's only thee
To bless my spirit now.
We used to love, on winter nights
To wander through the snow;
Can we not woo back old delights?
The clouds rush dark and wild
They flick with shade our mountain heights,
The same as long ago
And on the horizon rest at last
In looming masses piled;
While moonbeams flash and fly so fast
We scarce can say they smiled.

Come walk with me, come walk with me;
We were not once so few
But Death has stolen our company
As sunshine steals the dew.
He took them one by one and we
Are left the only two;
So closer would my feelings twine
Because they have no stay but mine.

"May call me not, it may not be
"Is human love so true?
"Can Friendship's flower droop on for years
"And then revive anew?
"No, though the soil be wet with tears
"How fair soe'er it grew
"The vital sap once perished
"will never flow again
"And surer than that dwelling dread,
"The narrow dungeon of the Dead,
"Time parts the hearts of men."

————

D⁺ 18   ✝ → a.B.h   O   E May 4ᵗʰ 1843

E Gᵒ to M.R.
A Serenade

Thy Guardians are asleep
So I'm come to bid thee rise;
Thou hast a holy vow to keep
Ere yon crescent quit the skies:

Though clouds careering wide,
will hardly let her gleam
She's bright enough to be our guide
Across the mountain stream.

EMILY BRONTË

A Peculiar Music

POEMS FOR YOUNG READERS
CHOSEN, INTRODUCED AND ANNOTATED BY
NAOMI LEWIS

THE MACMILLAN COMPANY
NEW YORK, NEW YORK

We are grateful to the Columbia University Press for permission to reprint the poems in this selection from *The Complete Poems of Emily Jane Brontë* edited from the manuscripts by C. W. Hatfield, 1941. The main source of most of the poems reprinted here are the two notebooks 'discovered' by Charlotte in 1845. One notebook is headed 'Gondal Poems': this is now in the British Museum, and a page from it is reproduced here by permission of the Trustees. The other is available only in facsimile versions made earlier in this century: the original (in private hands) seems at the moment untraced.

First published in Great Britain by The Bodley Head Ltd. 1971
This selection, introduction and notes Copyright © 1971 Naomi Lewis

The Macmillan Company, 866 Third Avenue, New York, N.Y. 10022
Library of Congress catalog card number: 75-178597
Printed in the United States of America

10   9   8   7   6   5   4   3   2   1

Contents

INTRODUCTION

Emily Brontë's short mysterious life (1818–1848), with its few
apparent events, and its fewer human links outside her own
family, seems as open as the moors; it is also as secret.
Probing studies of what she did and what she wrote increase
all the time; fresh discoveries—facts and texts—are still being
made. Yet the answering of any one question appears only to
open another. Everything in her story seems touched by
paradox and chance. Even the essential Yorkshire setting
came from the accident of a clergyman father's appointment.
The Brontës' father was Irish-born, the mother Cornish.
Emily Brontë did not look for public acclaim, and she
certainly did not get it in her lifetime. Yet today, wherever
books are read in the world, she ranks as a peak figure.
Writing was her passionate occupation from childhood on-
wards—yet all that survives today is a single novel and a
group of poems; her whole reputation rests on these. If her
other manuscripts were destroyed, as they must have been,
whose hand put them on the flames? Her own, most likely.
And yet if this is so, the destruction, and the preserving of
what we have, are interlinked; without the one, we would not
have had the other.

Her very appearance hovers on the eluding side of chance.
How tantalising to think that, living until December 1848,
she might just have been caught by those early, excellent
photographers. Her father was actually so recorded, thirteen
years later. As it is, we have only a few uncertain portraits—
practice work of her brother when still hardly more than a
boy. Branwell's brief career as a painter, like everything else

he tried, lapsed into nothing. Yet Branwell was also a
Brontë, and something comes through from the canvases—
not so much a physical likeness as an intense impression. If all
his work had been as inspired as the profile reproduced on
the jacket of this book, his name might too have lived on its
own.

And why are there not more verbal descriptions? It
should have been easy to gather them. At least Charlotte's
school friend Ellen Nussey, later a frequent visitor to the
parsonage, did not fail in this. She remembered Emily as 'a
lithesome, graceful figure':

> She was the tallest person in the house, except her father
> . . . She had very beautiful eyes—kind, kindling, liquid
> eyes; but she did not often look at you: she was too
> reserved. Their colour might be said to be dark grey, at
> other times dark blue, they varied so. She talked very little.
> She and Anne were like twins—inseparable companions,
> and in the very closest sympathy, which never had any
> interruption.

Such was Emily at 15; it might have described her (and her
link with Anne—the one friend she allowed) at any time.
Thin, restless, long-legged, unsociable, indifferent to the
worst of weathers, she was hardly a fashionable girl in an age
when the young Queen Victoria, small and round, was the
feminine model. Letters and anecdotes show Emily as clever,
reserved, self-sufficient, impatient of fuss and sentiment, but
in the easy setting of home she could be both amused and
amusing—certainly she was not till the end of her days (and
then for several good reasons) the awesome figure of legend.
It is true that she preferred to avoid encountering strangers
and unfamiliar scenes ('Charlotte will tell me,' she was
inclined to say); that, sharing the family devotion to animals,
she preferred those 'of a wild fierce intractability of nature'
(Mrs Gaskell's phrase). Like the heroine of Charlotte's
novel *Shirley*—a character based on Emily—she would sit on

the rug reading, 'with her arms round her rough bull-dog's neck'. If we did not know elsewhere of the value she set on liberty and on independent thought (things hard enough to achieve in her time, for a woman specially), and on stoical courage, we should learn these things from her poems. Yet the four surviving diary letters found in her papers—they are reproduced at the end of this book—show an almost light-hearted girl, hopeful and forward-looking, never grim and intense. She may well have been surprised at last by the force of her own achievement. But then, she had never written for outside effect or for critical praise. Left to herself she might have reached the end of her life without allowing a single other human (her sister Anne excepted, perhaps) to see her work. At the same time, left to herself she might not have given us *Wuthering Heights*.

Emily Jane Brontë was the fifth of six children, all born within seven years. Before her, came Maria, Elizabeth, Charlotte, and Branwell (the only boy); after her, Anne. She was about a year and a half when the family made the cumbrous journey from Thornton to Haworth—her father's last change of parsonage—and three when her mother died after many long months of illness. Aunt Branwell, poor Mrs Brontë's older sister, came dutifully from Cornwall to manage the household, and stayed there for the rest of her life. She was orderly, prim, and detached—no bad thing that. But the 'mother' whom the Brontës would always remember, the protecting spirit of their earliest years, was not an adult at all. She was their sister Maria. This grave and gifted little girl, undoubtedly touched by the family genius, would take the five small children out on the moors; she would read to them from serious books and newspapers—whatever might be found in the house—and was a fount of gentle wisdom and advice. A rare guardianship—but it was soon to end. For, in the late spring of 1825, Maria was dead, and Elizabeth too; the one not yet twelve years old, the other not yet eleven.

9

Their fragile constitutions could not stand up to the harsh conditions of the 'charitable' school to which all the girls except the baby Anne had recently been sent—the Clergy Daughters' School at Cowan Bridge. Years later, Charlotte's burning anger would be expressed in print; the school lives on as Lowood in *Jane Eyre*.

Actual remembrances of the two oldest children, Maria and Elizabeth, are so rare that the much-quoted 'mask' story (first set down in Mrs Gaskell's Life of Charlotte) might well be recounted here. Though the father was a very old man when he related the episode, the very strangeness of its detail seems to put it past invention; and we cannot doubt that it is intrinsically true to the nature of those closely-allied yet differing characters.

When my children were very young, [Patrick Brontë wrote] when, as far as I can remember, the oldest was about ten years of age, and the youngest about four, thinking that they knew more than I had yet discovered, in order to make them speak with less timidity, I deemed that if they were put under a sort of cover I might gain my end; and happening to have a mask in the house, I told them all to stand and speak boldly from under cover of the mask.

I began with the youngest (Anne, afterwards Acton Bell), and asked what a child like her most wanted; she answered, 'Age and experience.' I asked the next (Emily, afterwards Ellis Bell), what I had best do with her brother Branwell, who was sometimes a naughty boy; she answered, 'Reason with him, and when he won't listen to reason, whip him.' I asked Branwell what was the best way of knowing the difference between the intellects of man and woman; he answered, 'By considering the difference between them as to their bodies.' I then asked Charlotte what was the best book in the world; she answered, 'The Bible.' And what was the next best; she answered, 'The

Book of Nature.' I then asked the next what was the best mode of education for a woman; she answered, 'That which would make her rule her house well.' Lastly, I asked the oldest what was the best mode of spending time; she answered, 'By laying it out in preparation for a happy eternity.' I may not have given precisely their words, but I have nearly done so, as they made a deep and lasting impression on my memory. The substance, however, was exactly what I have stated.

Emily too had been at Cowan Bridge school, but the younger ones, perhaps, had been under kindlier care. A teacher ('Miss Temple' of *Jane Eyre*) described her to Mrs Gaskell as 'a darling child, quite the pet nursling of the school'. There is a note about her in the records:

Emily Brontë. Entered Nov. 25, 1824. Aged 5¾. Reads very prettily and works a little. Left June 1, 1825. Subsequent career, governess.

Inaccurate on age (and career) but not without interest. As a little girl, Emily was no miniature Heathcliff, surly and menacing.

And now, as the children reassembled at home, Charlotte, formerly third in age, found herself in the leader's role. Imagination was her particular quality, as wisdom had been Maria's, and, before long—sparked off by the father's present to Branwell of a box of wooden soldiers—a number of dramatic games were started. First they were 'played' or acted out; then they began to be put on paper.

Our plays were established [Charlotte wrote a few years later]: *Young Men*, June 1826; *Our Fellows*, July 1827; *Islanders*, December 1827. These are our three great plays, they are not kept secret. Emily's and my best plays were established the 1st of December, 1827; the others, March, 1828. Best plays mean secret plays; they are very nice ones. All our plays are very strange ones.

In Charlotte's early papers these beginnings are set out in remarkably vivid detail. We seem in the very room as each child chooses and names a soldier ('Emily's was a grave-looking fellow and we called him "Gravey"'); we feel the warmth of the firelit kitchen when—since old Tabby will not allow them a candle to read by—each child selects an island, and peoples it with famous characters. Emily's was Arran; one of her 'chief men' Sir Walter Scott. In June 1826, we may note, she was not quite eight years old.

But the plays were not only 'strange'; they were immensely powerful, channelling all the reading, ideas and tireless invention of the close-knit, gifted four. The torrent at length divided into two main streams: sagas of two imaginary kingdoms—Angria, chronicled by Charlotte and Branwell, and Gondal, a breakaway creation of Emily and Anne, begun when Charlotte left for a new school, Roe Head, in 1831. The alliance of Charlotte and Emily, described in the first note, had been brief. The alliance of Emily and Anne, however, was to last through life. All of them set down their tales in a tiny print-like script (partly to imitate print itself, partly since paper was scarce and dear); the pages were then made up into little books, some not much larger than match-box size. No stranger's eyes (except, quickly and casually, those of Mrs Gaskell) were to read the Angrian stories for the best part of a century. No stranger's eyes have ever seen the Gondal stories. An extraordinary fact! For Emily was still writing within this framework until three years before she died. Yet every Gondal book has gone without a trace.

How, then, do we know of Gondal at all? For we do, indeed, know something of its characters, and even more of its landscape and atmosphere. The evidence seems at first quite plentiful. Thus, in a geography book we find a list of Gondal place-names in Anne's writing, among them:

Gondal, a large Island in the North Pacific.
Gaaldine, a large Island newly discovered in the South Pacific.
Ula, a kingdom in Gaaldine, governed by 4 Sovereigns.

Then, written by Emily on the edge of one of her own poetry manuscripts, is a list of names of persons—Gondal characters—with descriptive detail set out in a kind of code.

All the diary letters exchanged with Anne (pp. 79–85) give lively mentions of the Gondal stories that both are currently working on; indeed, it was a sentence in the first of these ('The Gondals are discovering the interior of Gaaldine'—followed immediately by 'Sally Mosley is washing in the back-kitchin') that started the great tide of modern detective-work on the mystery.

As for the poems themselves, they are full of tantalising hints and clues. From all these tracts and traces numbers of writers have tried to reconstruct the story. But the versions differ; perhaps we shall never know the full solution. It is almost as if we have the key but the door cannot be found. Yet the nature of Gondal itself is clear enough—a northern land of ancient halls, wild winds and drifting snows, peopled by dark, heroic, tragic characters: warriors, troubadours, children of princely houses.

> How gloomy grows the night! 'Tis Gondal's wind that
>   blows;
> I shall not tread again the deep glens where it rose—
> I feel it on my face—'Where, wild blast, dost thou roam?
> 'What do we, wanderer, here, so far away from home?'

This verse from a poem dated November 1, 1838, when she was probably herself 'in exile' from the parsonage, powerfully suggests the Gondal mood but it also reminds us that—for all its castles out of Ossian and Walter Scott and its denizens out of Byron—Gondal was quintessentially Emily's own idealised moorland country: lovely in summer (see p. 37) but unsurpassed in its appeal in night and winter.

Fancy took her at will to the moors of Gondal; but in fact, apart from that early Cowan Bridge sojourn and a few brief local excursions, Emily went away from Haworth on only three occasions. Each of these arose from the need for the girls to equip themselves to be teachers or governesses, a need which they all accepted. They could hardly do less. For if the father died, the parsonage home would also go—and what other way was there to earn a living? And so, in 1835, Emily went as pupil to the Miss Woolers' school at Roe Head. It was there that Charlotte, at 14, had first met Mary Taylor and Ellen Nussey, who became her lifelong friends. But Emily never chose to make friends. Like a caged wild bird she drooped and pined—and after three months came home. Two years later she bravely set out again—now as a teacher—to Law Hill, 'a large school' (in Charlotte's words) 'of near forty pupils, near Halifax'; she stayed perhaps as long as a year and a half—the exact time is still disputed. But several poems, including *A little while* and *Loud without the wind was roaring* clearly describe a mood of these prisoned days.

After these two unhappy experiments, how ever did she come to consent to a third and by far the most distant project —a year to be spent in Belgium? But Charlotte's persuasive power, as we shall see again, was never to be discounted in the Brontës' story. The sisters were considering a plan to start a small school of their own at the parsonage; to equip them-selves for this, a period abroad, studying languages, seemed essential. So in 1842 we find the two older Brontë girls setting out for the Pensionnat Heger in Brussels, a school to which Charlotte would once again give lasting fictional life, in *The Professor* and *Villette*. For Charlotte, especially, it would give the longed-for chance to see the buildings and paintings and to hear the music performed, that could only be known by hearsay in a remote Yorkshire village. Remember that this was before the time of reproduced sound (no radio, no records) or pictures. In November, however, the death of Aunt Branwell brought both girls back to Haworth; there-after, Emily was never troubled to go from home again.

Of Emily's view of the Brussels experience, not a word can be found. We know very well how much it meant to Charlotte, both before and after, but Emily's thoughts remain a total enigma. She had worked hard to learn—it was the reason for her going. (A few of her essays in French have recently turned up.) But here too, she made no friends. She had nothing in common with the fashionable older girls; the young ones to whom she was asked to teach music thought her distant and formidable. Nothing in Emily's poetry, nothing in *Wuthering Heights* would suggest that she had spent many months in a great foreign city (with some extra sightseeing days in London while the boat awaited a tide). But the complete break from northern England must have given her, for the first time, a perspective view of her own particular scene. The novelist tends to need this where the poet does not. And in Brussels, most likely, the idea of *Wuthering Heights*, her first story set on the Yorkshire soil, with 'modern', not Gondal characters, must have taken root.

As for the impression that Emily left—a matter of no less interest—one famous comment has come down, from the school's principal, Professor Heger himself. Years later, when the Brontës were famous and dead, he looked back on the shy, difficult English girl, whom he had thought at first both timid and obstinate. If she had been a man, he wrote, she would have been 'a great navigator. Her powerful reason would have deduced new spheres of discovery from her knowlege of the old; and her strong imperious will would never have been daunted by opposition or difficulty; never have given way but with life.'

On her return, Emily must have felt at last a rare freedom to work; she had much to work upon. At this very time, between 1843 and 1845, her sisters and brother were feeling increasingly restless, bruised and despondent. All had been in the world, and had found themselves no match for it; every hopeful road to the future seemed blocked. Emily alone seemed happily occupied and content. Her busy life at home, with its housework, washing and breadmaking, was austere and disciplined enough, but it contained in its solitude the freedom of mind that she could not do without. The effect of other disciplines than her own was like death, because they cut her off from this essential freedom. The diary letters exchanged between Anne and Emily on July 31, 1845 (to be opened three years later) present a striking contrast. Anne reports that she has had 'some very unpleasant and undreamt-of experiences of human nature'. She had indeed! She had just returned from her final governess post in the disastrous house where Branwell, also engaged there as tutor, had been almost destroyed by a passion (not discouraged) for his employer's wife. (See Mrs Gaskell for this.) Sadly Anne concludes: 'I for my part cannot well be flatter or older in mind than I am now.'

How different is Emily's vigorous note. She describes a recent expedition to York with Anne ('our first long journey by ourselves together'), and the Gondal stories they worked out on the way. 'The Gondals still flourish bright as ever,' she writes. She describes how the school plan had fallen through, and the general unspoken relief. 'Now I don't desire a school at all and none of us have any great longing for it.' (Aunt Branwell's small legacy allowed a welcome pause.) She even hopes that Branwell (already drinking himself to death) will 'be better and do better hereafter'. 'I am quite contented for myself,' she adds, '—not as idle as formerly, altogether as hearty, seldom or ever troubled with nothing to do, merely desiring that every body could be as comfortable as myself and as undesponding and then we should have a very tolerable world of it.' She goes on to tell what has happened to all the birds and animals, old and new; she speaks of the black-currants that need to be picked, and ends, 'I must hurry off now to my turning and ironing. I have plenty of work on hands, and writing, and am altogether full of business. With best wishes for the whole house till 1848, July 30th, and as much longer as may be.'

Simple enough, but startling from the Emily Brontë of legend, imagined as darkly striding the hills like one of her own wild Gondals. Certainly, she did not know how ominous that future date would be, nor that this was her final diary note. She was, however, at this very time writing the most profound, most searching and most mysterious of all her poems; she was already deeply involved in *Wuthering Heights*. How can we explain her mood of energy, peace and gaiety even? We have to remember that when creative work goes well, the heart lifts. The peculiar exhilaration of finding words to voice what is almost inexpressible can irradiate the most ordinary details of everyday life (an experience described, in a different context, by George Herbert), and Emily was now at the very height of her gift.

But the poems—and even the prose, no doubt—were essentially private utterances and Emily's power as a writer lay in this. A few weeks after the diary note was written, a curious happening would bring the secret, sustaining course to an end. Charlotte describes the event in a memorable passage.

One day, in the autumn of 1845, I accidentally lighted on a MS volume of verse, in my sister Emily's handwriting. Of course, I was not surprised, knowing that she could and did write verse: I looked it over, and something more than surprise seized me—a deep conviction that these were not common effusions, nor at all like the poetry women generally write. I thought them condensed and terse, vigorous and genuine. To my ear they had also a peculiar music— wild, melancholy and elevating.

My sister Emily was not a person of demonstrative character, nor one on the recesses of whose mind and feelings even those nearest and dearest to her could, with impunity, intrude unlicensed; it took hours to reconcile her to the discovery I had made, and days to persuade her that such poems merited publication. I knew, however, that a mind like hers could not be without some latent spark of honourable ambition, and refused to be discouraged in my attempts to fan that spark to flame.

We can imagine the scene. What Charlotte had found was one of the two small notebooks in which Emily had begun to copy out neatly what she felt were the best of her completed poems. Both books were dated February 1844; one was given the heading *Gondal Poems*; the other was evidently for those more directly personal. Emily *was* persuaded; it was not the first time that Charlotte's kindling power had performed this near-miracle. Each sister provided a choice of poems (Emily carefully removing all Gondal references); pseudonyms (not obtrusively masculine) were decided on; a publisher was found (requiring a contribution of just over £30), and in May 1846, *Poems* by Currer, Ellis and Acton Bell appeared. These dedicated writers, who for so long had made, bound and print-scripted their own tiny books, had achieved real print at last. The few reviews were favourable; Emily's poems were singled out as original, possibly heralding 'things to speak that men will be glad to hear'. Never mind that only two copies were sold (to whom? one often wonders); new light, new plans had entered the parsonage. Each sister wrote the last words to a novel, copied it neatly out by hand, and the parcels were sent out to publishers.

Even Emily must have caught something of Charlotte's fiery hope. A degree of curiosity could hardly help mingling with the resistance. But the notebooks received only two more poems. *No coward soul is mine*, dated January 1846, could well have been in Emily's thoughts for some time. There was also, however, one strange last Gondal poem (*Why ask to know the date—the clime?*) in rapid 4-iambic couplets, about the debasing effects of war not only on the victims and the countryside but on those who wield the sword. This grim and passionate narrative, not at all in the mood of earlier Brontë heroics, was dated September 14, 1846; in the May of 1848 it was briefly taken up again and dropped—the last thing, as far as we know, that Emily ever wrote.

At the end of 1845, the 'discovery' year, Emily had just three more years to live. They were eventful years in the household. She would witness the brilliant, soaring success of Charlotte's *Jane Eyre* (published in the autumn of 1847) and the last black months of Branwell, the family failure, too deranged by drink to know that the longed-for literary triumph had come at last to the Brontë home. She would see —with mixed feelings—her own novel in print. For *Wuthering Heights* was carelessly produced, after long delays, by a corrupt and dilatory publisher, trying to make dishonest use of Charlotte's reflected glory. It was not ignored by reviewers and readers, but it was neither understood nor truly valued in Emily's lifetime, nor long after that.

It is strange that, when the Brontës come most into the open, when outside observers begin to be on the alert, Emily appears most shadowy. She had no wish for the identity of Ellis Bell to be known. Was she, like her sisters, at work on another novel? There is a possible clue that she was. But, if so, it was destroyed with her other prose stories and its subject is beyond our power to guess at.

Could she still move into the Gondal Kingdom? Or were its gates entirely closed? It had begun as a child's daydream— but the child was no ordinary dreamer. As she grew, Gondal advanced with her, a great terrain in which the special aspects of life which interested her could be endlessly studied and played out—endurance, self-sufficiency, the relations of humans with nature (birds, beasts, plants, the harebell and the heather, wind and snow, the elements and the seasons), the passionate reach of imagination—and memory, visionary experiences, the implications of death. What this kingdom could not take was the intrusive daylight, the stare of strangers' eyes. As soon as even a part of it—the notebook of poems—had come into the open, its special enchantment must have gone. No doubt the manuscripts themselves, the marvelous hoard of tiny books, began to go soon after this—though about their actual destruction, all records are utterly silent.

And yet—it is probably fair to say that the best of Emily's work is in what remains. If Gondal had not been interrupted,

Wuthering Heights might never have been completed. If the poems had not been found and fixed in print, they might well have disappeared with the prose chronicles: the same play of chance and paradox. The work of a highly gifted life cut short has almost always a sense of added pace and tension, and it could well be that all that was important for Emily Brontë to say, had been said. By luck, we can read it still.

Did she open the buoyant diary letters, due to be looked at on her July birthday in 1848? Quite possibly, yes. But, significantly, neither she nor Anne appear to have written another. By the end of that year, she was dead. A cold caught at Branwell's funeral, late in September, had roused the latent tubercular tendencies that must have been in all the family. Now, at last, too much like the awesome Emily of legend, she rejected doctors; she rejected the fact of illness itself. Medical help of those days could have done nothing; but rest itself might have prolonged her days. Death, of course, was not new to her; the very churchyard lay just outside the door. Mother, sisters, brother, youthful family friends (like Martha Taylor, and the charming curate Willie Weightman) had gone: cholera and consumption seemed to prefer the young. But we can never be sure if she was setting her powerful will against life or death. She seems at the end to have, at the same time, lost and won.

By the mid-century, all the Brontë sisters were dead (Anne died of tuberculosis, in May 1849, Charlotte seven years later). But their reputation was only at the beginning of its course. How (many readers reflected) did the three shy unworldly shortlived sisters produce a group of fully-fledged brilliant novels, as absorbing to men as to women? What experiences lay behind the remarkable poems and fiction? Emily, as the most secret, enigmatic and disturbing, became the chief prey of emotional, literary guesswork. One headlong author, misreading a pencilled title 'Love's Farewell' as Louis Parensell, gave an embroidered account of this person as Emily's secret flame. To the 'popular' biographer, few characters can be more baffling than the contented solitary, not a 'religious', indifferent to ordinary human relationships, pursuing only the course of his (or her) own gift. No wonder that the dramatic Gondal ballads of passion and death and burials on the moor were seized on as straight personal documents. And yet—it is not usually assumed that, when Shakespeare wrote *Macbeth*, he had previously arranged to murder a king. He did, of course, know much about the force of human ambition—and also about the bitter taste that its forced fulfilment all too often brings.

What almost nobody knew, was how much practice as novelists the Brontës had had from childhood, how many wild romantic themes (touched off by early reading of Byron, Scott, the *Arabian Nights*, by local scenes and legends, even) they had worked through before their known adult books appeared. The evidence was there—all the time—but hidden through the Victorian years in an Irish farmhouse. To track the story, we have to go back to 1861, when the last surviving Brontë at Haworth Parsonage died. This was the father, the Reverend Patrick, and with the old man's death the tenure of the place came to an end. But an heir remained, in the parsonage itself, and as closely concerned as a blood relative might have been—Charlotte's husband, the Reverend Arthur Nicholls. Sharing the lonely house with Mr Brontë, still as curate, he had also taken on most of the work of the church as well. When his father-in-law was gone, and a new incumbent was, not very fairly, appointed over his head, Arthur Nicholls packed and left for his native Ireland, taking with him all portable treasures and documents. There he lived quietly, resisting publicity hunters, until, almost incredibly, 1906.

Mr Nicholls remains one of the most tantalising characters in the story. He had been appointed curate at Haworth in 1845; he must have seen the sisters constantly, and informally, during the most significant years of their lives. His marriage with Charlotte, though short, was a happy one; we could even say that he had proved to be more like the romantic and dominating Mr Rochester than Charlotte had ever expected. After her death he had spent six years with old Mr Brontë, facing the barrage of information-seekers. And he had inherited—everything: all papers, pictures and documents. He must have known the answers to almost all the questions that still vex students of Brontë-lore; he must have been able to give a unique personal impression of each of the family. Surely he must have spoken at times of these things, at least to friends, in the last fifty years of his life? But if there *are* any records of conversations, they have not come to light. He had loved Charlotte, and hated the Brontë-cult, and to all outsiders preferred to be silent.

But there was to be a break at last in the barrier and this we owe to an enterprising London editor and Brontë enthusiast Clement Shorter. Looking up Charlotte's will to see how the law stood about certain unpublished letters, he had become aware of the one quiet survivor, and contrived to win Mr Nicholls' confidence. Perhaps the unworldly old man was beginning to wonder what *should* be done with the documents. In 1895 Shorter travelled to Ireland and came back with a great pile of papers that had been gathering dust in a cupboard. This priceless haul included most of the known manuscripts of Emily's poems; and, in a tin box, the folded scraps of diary letters, that have done so much to illuminate and yet confuse the portrait of Emily. There were no Gondal stories, alas, but the Angrian saga (the work of Charlotte and Branwell) was there, in hundreds of tiny books —as were almost all of Charlotte's writings before *Jane Eyre*.

Shorter made careful copies (which was good)—then (which was not so good) put most of the originals into the salerooms, to be bought by wealthy collectors all over the world. It was to take the first important researcher, an American librarian, Miss Fanny Ratchford, many years to track them down (some, as the notes will show, are still untraced) and to study the miniature stories. Her resulting book *The Brontës' Web of Childhood* (1941)—a real literary landmark—

a..d the researches of later scholars and biographers (notably Winifred Gérin who has written full-length separate books on each of the family) have, one hopes, for ever ended the wild assertions made, in books, on the Brontës' lives and loves. Stage and cinema writers, though, seem to feel less need to be scrupulous. Odd—for the truth has turned out to be stranger than all the guess-work.

But Gondal is far from being the total answer to the mystery of Emily Brontë's genius. A poem of hers may begin in a Gondal setting, like a day dream set on paper, then suddenly serve as a frame for some riveting personal statement, a poem within a poem. The change in tempo and depth can be startling. The outstanding instance of this is the marvellous seven-verse passage in the long poem *Julian M. and A. G. Rochelle*—the prisoner's 'mystical' experience which was undoubtedly Emily's too. But the moors of Gondal and the moors of Yorkshire are not really so far apart—perhaps not apart at all. Emily's whole life and her work are linked in this same way; each adds to and draws from the quality of the other. So, nothing in the simplicity of her days ever seems quite trivial. So too, whatever path we take through her work or life, we come back richer, not quite the same as we were. When Cathy in *Wuthering Heights* declares:

'I've dreamed in my life dreams that have stayed with me ever after, and changed my ideas; they've gone through and through me, like wine through water, and altered the colour of my mind'—

she is speaking not only for herself but for her author, and not only for her author but for those who read her work. Indeed, the more we look into Emily Brontë's strange and magical poems, the further we advance into her rare imagination. Certain mysteries have no absolute answer, but are endlessly valuable to explore. And the problems posed by Emily Brontë's writings belong with these. She had to an extraordinary degree the power that goes beyond its own intention: perhaps (especially when it creates what is valuable) this is one of the definitions of genius. Because she possessed it, we are able to share, in lightning moments of prose and verse, something of her own unique and haunting vision.

Wishes when greatly wished have a way of coming about, though they also have their price; they have, moreover, just the limit or scope of their wisher's capacity. That is one of the major lessons of fairy tale, and it holds true for adult and child alike. Charlotte was to achieve, in her lifetime, the high fame that she had longed for, and surely earned—but at pain and cost. Emily did not want the regard of the world she lived in. An early fragment suggests the range of her desire.

> I'm happiest when most away
> I can bear my soul from its home of clay
> On a windy night when the moon is bright
> And the eye can wander through worlds of light—
>
> When I am not and none beside—
> Nor earth nor sea nor cloudless sky—
> But only spirit wandering wide
> Through infinite immensity.

Yet the earthly landscape about her meant immeasurably much, as her poems continually show. Her novel reveals that she likewise saw very clearly the *peopled* scene, though she did not wish for its company or its praise. In her poem *How beautiful the Earth is still* (p.69) where she speaks of rejecting fame she notes that the sands are effaced by the waves, but the sea (always her symbol for the infinite) endures. There, in those 'enduring seas' she would cast her 'anchor of Desire, deep in unknown Eternity'. That may well be the kind of time she is likely to bridge. She seems, with unflinching logic, to have done her best to efface the print of her steps from the sands or snow of her days, but her essential gift lives on. It can hardly be more strikingly and rewardingly encountered than in the best of the poems from which this choice is made.

NAOMI LEWIS

THE POEMS

Just under 200 poems or fragments of poems by Emily
Brontë (193, at current counting) are known to us today.
Luckily, whatever else may have been destroyed, the two
notebooks into which she copied the best of her poetry (set
down in her tiny script with a not quite sharp enough quill
pen which sometimes thickens the letters) have survived. So it
is reasonable to suppose that we *have* the best that she wrote.
But we also have much that survives only by accident: early
experiments, misfires, youthful Gondal fantasies like day-
dreams on the page. Sometimes, when the spark went out,
she would leave a poem mid-way, or turn it without a pause
into another. Selection, then, is not so much a matter of
choosing favourites as of sifting out practice work that she
herself would certainly not have passed or even preserved. It
is important to remember that she was not writing for other
critical eyes. Her sister Anne, who naturally knew the Gondal
stories, must also have seen a number of the poems—at any
rate, the earlier and less personal ones. But Anne could not be
largely objective; she was, after all, a writer of much the same
kind, with roots in the same ground. This complete isolation
from criticism, or from critical exchange—extremely rare in
a poet of Emily's quality—was in some ways a disadvantage;
but—*because* of her quality—it was, as she progressed, an
ultimate source of power.

Anyone reading Emily Brontë's poems for the first time is
likely to have several prompt and possibly contradictory
impressions. One is of something urgent, hurrying, forceful,
swift in the formal verses—'condensed energy' in Charlotte's
admirable phrase. There is a pervading sense of atmosphere—

25

a meeting of wild landscape and wild elements. The metres and manner, on the other hand, seem curiously simple—so many ballad quatrains or rhyming couplets. Then, looked at again, they do not seem simple at all; there is a continual freedom and variation within the lines themselves. Often, they do not even *sound* like other poetry of their time. *Cold in the earth, and the deep snow piled above thee . . . Cold in the earth, and fifteen wild Decembers . . . Death, that struck when I was most confiding.* Single, more regular lines arrest us: *Light up thy halls! 'Tis closing day . . . And like myself lone, wholly lone . . . Or would I mock the wolf's death-howl | Because his form is gaunt and foul?* And all those beginning with the defiant, conversational 'Well—'; *Well, some may hate, and some may scorn*—straightway we are caught by the attack. The most surprising metre belongs to *Julian M. and A. G. Rochelle*, which must be one of the most haunting poems in the language.

> He comes with western winds, with evening's wandering airs,
> With that clear dusk of heaven that brings the thickest stars;
> Winds take a pensive tone, and stars a tender fire,
> And visions rise and change which kill me with desire—

Yet what is behind its racing light mysterious sound but the old 6-iambic, the alexandrine, usually thought of as pompous, ponderous, slow!

Noticeably, Emily Brontë never tries out the sonnet or other intricate verse forms that nearly every poet has practised at some time. There are plenty, even, in Emily's admired Byron. One feels, though, that the tune in her head (and everyone who has ever written a poem will know what this means) was usually carried along by a theme too immediate and intense for, say, the sonnet or the Spenserian stanza—the form, by the way, of such essentially romantic poems as *Childe Harold, Adonais,* and *The Eve of St Agnes.*

At the same time, it is clear enough that she *could* follow the echo of some particular measure, if it appealed to her; several poems quite vividly suggest, for instance, a background of plucked-string music. One of these is the harp poem in the present selection. There is also the delicate fragment below, with its authentic air of a seventeenth-century lyric.

> Fall, leaves, fall; die, flowers, away;
> Lengthen night and shorten day;
> Every leaf speaks bliss to me
> Fluttering from the autumn tree.
> I shall smile when wreaths of snow
> Blossom where the rose should grow;
> I shall sing when night's decay
> Ushers in a drearier day.

Even more effective, of this kind, is a Gondal dialogue poem *In the earth, the earth*; for all its Brontëan flavour, it could equally well be a true Shakespearean lute-song. Here are its opening and closing verses:

> In the earth, the earth, thou shalt be laid,
> A grey stone standing over thee;
> Black mould beneath thee spread
> And black mould to cover thee.
>
> 'Well, there is rest there,
> So fast come thy prophecy;
> The time when my sunny hair
> Shall with grass roots twinèd be.' . . .
>
> Farewell, then, all that love,
> All that deep sympathy;
> Sleep on; heaven laughs above,
> Earth never misses thee.

Poetry does not grow out of nothing. Great or small, epic or doggerel, lyric or nursery rhyme, it has its ancestors no less than a man or a plant; rebellion itself admits the existence of what is rebelled against. Poets hear language around them, catch echoes of popular rhymes and songs and other patterns of words and sounds, not always knowing even that they have encountered them. But, above all, they read other poets. Which poetry reached the young Brontës at Haworth? Certainly, and influentially, Shakespeare, Cowper, Burns, Ossian (reviewed by Branwell in a childish, Brontëan magazine), Coleridge, Wordsworth, and the recent and romantic Byron and Scott. The two last made a particular mark. There is no sign that Emily ever knew the poems of Keats; but she must at some time (probably when in her twenties) have read Shelley, a poet whose view of man and nature, especially elemental nature, is often so much in key with her own. She also knew, from an early age, the old northern ballads and, of course, a range of Methodist hymns; unlike as they may seem, they have not a little in common in their strong simple passionate statements and strong resounding words. Both these features are found in her own verse. But out of the apprenticeship comes the original voice, and Emily Brontë's is unmistakable.

'Nature'—landscape, weather, seasons, grassblade, snow-flake, bird and leaf—has an essential part in Emily Brontë's poems. Yet she is not, like Clare for instance, truly in the English Nature tradition. Though she observes with absolute fidelity the brown heather, the 'blue ice curdling on the stream', though she never uses these things as background, merely, or decoration (there are almost no similes in her work, by the way), yet they seem to belong more to an inner landscape, than to a directly-recorded scene. Of this inner scene she herself is a part, on the same terms, almost, as tree and plant and bird. Charlotte's note in the 1850 Preface makes the point very plainly:

> Ellis Bell did not describe as one whose eye and taste alone found pleasure in the prospect; her native hills were far more to her than a spectacle; they were what she lived in, and by, as much as the wild birds, their tenants, or as the heather, their produce.

The result is a strange one; nature—whatever its aspects in

the poem—intensely affects the poem's tempo and character:
its 'peculiar music', one might say. An attractive illustration
is the sudden close of a long and leisured poem *Written in
Aspin Castle*, begun in Brussels and finished a month or two
after Emily's return to Haworth. Here, the ecstasy of home-
coming is contained in the ecstasy of the night.

> O come away! the Norman door
> Is silvered with a sudden shine;
> Come, leave these dreams o'er things of yore
> And turn to Nature's face divine.
>
> O'er wood and wold, o'er flood and fell,
> O'er flashing lake and gleaming dell,
> The harvest moon looks down;
> And when heaven smiles with love and light,
> And earth looks back so dazzling bright—
> In such a scene, on such a night,
> Earth's children should not frown.

A verse from another poem (part of which is reproduced
opposite the title-page of this volume) shows, almost disturb-
ingly, how the human and the elemental increasingly gain in
pace and excitement each from the other. Notice, too, that
however much the whole thing may be taken as a metaphor—
most poems are this, after all—there are no comparisons:
cloud, moonbeam and the rest appear as themselves.

> Come, walk with me,
> There's only thee
> To bless my spirit now;
> We used to love on winter nights
> To wander through the snow;
> Can we not woo back old delights?
> The clouds rush dark and wild;
> They fleck with shade our mountain heights
> The same as long ago,

And on the horizon rest at last
In looming masses piled;
While moonbeams flash and fly so fast
We scarce can say they smiled.

Nature affects no less the desolation of 'Cold in the earth, and
the deep snow piled above thee', and the remorseless beat of
the poem about the ill-starred boy:

Heavy looms the dull sky,
Heavy rolls the sea—
And heavy beats the young heart
Beneath that lonely tree.

But there are almost as many examples, sombre or light, as
there are poems in this book.

About her place in the poetic hierarchy, critics have never
come to any satisfactory conclusion. Major-minor? Minor-
major? These valuations seem not to be relevant. A solitary
in life, she is also a solitary among the poets. Her work *is*
uneven—yet not a line of it fails to be stamped by her
arresting personality. And no one questions the greatness of
her great poems—few though they are, some five or six
perhaps. I shall not name them; only offer readers the
interesting chance of hunting them out for themselves.

It might be noted that the time when she was writing—
roughly, the ten years between 1836 and 1846—was one of
those odd and nameless periods that lie between one age of
literary flowering and another. The great romantics of a
generation earlier—Keats, Shelley, Byron, Coleridge too—
were dead; the new young Victorians, Tennyson and Brown-
ing, were just beginning to show their work in print. John
Clare, alone, was writing away at the height of his strange
gift; but he was in an asylum, as much away from the chang-
ing world and current literary fashions as Emily herself. In
such conditions notable writers tend to write in strong if
narrow channels away from the main current: they may even

(like Emily Dickinson and Gerard Manley Hopkins) be ahead of the main stream. Emily Brontë had not the range nor the technical audacity of these two; her conception of poetry seems to have been different. But she too belongs among the originals.

All the evidence suggests that Emily never readily turned to prose for setting down or working out her deepest personal thoughts. The philosophic essays that she wrote (in French) for M. Heger were a forced, uncharacteristic task. Keats made letters an important extension of his poetry—not so Emily Brontë. We know that she rarely wrote letters at all; the two or three that survive could hardly be more brisk and practical. Even the secret diary notes reveal nothing of the spirit of the poems that she was working on at the time. In the last birthday letter of July 1845, Anne observed:

> Emily is engaged in writing the Emperor Julius's Life. She has read some of it, and I want very much to hear the rest. She is writing some poetry, too. I wonder what it is about?

Well might she have wondered. Emily was following, at her highest poetic level, the final conflicts and resolutions of her beliefs. At this point we can see how little the Gondal division came to matter in her poetry, how easily the Gondal framework could enclose an outstanding personal statement. Her intensely personal creed is not always easy to follow. It agrees with no accepted theological line. Readers tend to find in individual poems just what they wish to find, but if they are honest, they will not look for confirmation of an easy orthodoxy. Yet there are consistent strands running through her work; her belief in the place of temporal human life within lasting nature; her dazzling vision of eternity—one that had no use for the angel-inhabited heaven of popular comfort. The range of her unelaborate, unornamented lines is vast indeed. Nor did she ever waver in her sense of the god-like power of the creative imagination, which gives and demands entire liberty of the spirit—and, too, the stoic's fortitude, the unfailing 'courage to endure'. We can see why Charlotte said that the poems, when she met them first, stirred her heart 'like the sound of a trumpet'—these strange and stirring poems that lead so unpredictably (yet laying down so many clues) to *Wuthering Heights*. It is an extraordinary thing to realise, too, that they are the nearest thing to an autobiography that we have of one of the most enigmatic and uncompromising minds of genius in the whole of our literature.

N.L.

[1]

High waving heather, 'neath stormy blasts bending,
Midnight and moonlight and bright shining stars;
Darkness and glory rejoicingly blending,
Earth rising to heaven and heaven descending,
Man's spirit away from its drear dongeon sending,
Bursting the fetters and breaking the bars.

All down the mountain sides, wild forests lending
One mighty voice to the life-giving wind;
Rivers their banks in the jubilee rending,
Fast through the valleys a reckless course wending,
Wider and deeper their waters extending,
Leaving a desolate desert behind.

Shining and lowering and swelling and dying,
Changing for ever from midnight to noon;
Roaring like thunder, like soft music sighing,
Shadows on shadows advancing and flying,
Lightning-bright flashes the deep gloom defying,
Coming as swiftly and fading as soon.

December 13, 1836

All day I've toiled, but not with pain,
In learning's golden mine;
And now at eventide again
The moonbeams softly shine.

There is no snow upon the ground,
No frost on wind or wave;
The south wind blew with gentlest sound
And broke their icy grave.

'Tis sweet to wander here at night
To watch the winter die,
With heart as summer sunshine light
And warm as summer sky.

O may I never lose the peace
That lulls me gently now,
Though time should change my youthful face,
And years should shade my brow!

True to myself, and true to all,
May I be healthful still,
And turn away from passion's call,
And curb my own wild will.

probably spring, 1837

[3]

All hushed and still within the house;
Without—all wind and driving rain;
But something whispers to my mind,
Through rain and through the wailing wind,
    Never again.
Never again? Why not again?
Memory has power as real as thine.

probably spring, 1838

[4]

Harp of wild and dream-like strain,
When I touch thy strings,
Why dost thou repeat again
Long-forgotten things?

Harp, in other, earlier days,
I could sing to thee;
And not one of all my lays
Vexed my memory.

But now, if I awake a note
That gave me joy before,
Sounds of sorrow from thee float,
Changing evermore.

Yet, still steeped in memory's dyes,
They come sailing on,
Darkening all my summer skies,
Shutting out my sun.

probably May, 1838

[5]

Loud without the wind was roaring
   Through the waned autumnal sky;
Drenching wet, the cold rain pouring
   Spoke of stormy winters nigh.

All too like that dreary eve
Sighed within repining grief;
Sighed at first, but sighed not long—
Sweet—How softly sweet it came!
Wild words of an ancient song,
Undefined, without a name.

'It was spring, for the skylark was singing.'
   Those words, they awakened a spell—
They unlocked a deep fountain whose springing
   Nor Absence nor Distance can quell.

In the gloom of a cloudy November,
   They uttered the music of May;
They kindled the perishing ember
   Into fervour that could not decay.

Awaken on all my dear moorlands
   The wind in its glory and pride!
O call me from valleys and highlands
   To walk by the hill-river's side!

It is swelled with the first snowy weather;
   The rocks they are icy and hoar
And darker waves round the long heather
   And the fern-leaves are sunny no more.

There are no yellow-stars on the mountain,
The blue-bells have long died away
From the brink of the moss-bedded fountain,
From the side of the wintery brae—

But lovelier than corn-fields all waving
In emerald and scarlet and gold
Are the slopes where the north-wind is raving,
And the glens where I wandered of old.

'It was morning; the bright sun was beaming.'
How sweetly that brought back to me
The time when nor labour nor dreaming
Broke the sleep of the happy and free.

But blithely we rose as the dusk heaven
Was melting to amber and blue;
And swift were the wings to our feet given
While we traversed the meadows of dew,

For the moors, for the moors where the short grass
Like velvet beneath us should lie!
For the moors, for the moors where each high pass
Rose sunny against the clear sky!

For the moors where the linnet was trilling
Its song on the old granite stone;
Where the lark—the wild skylark was filling
Every breast with delight like its own.

What language can utter the feeling
That rose when, in exile afar,
On the brow of a lonely hill kneeling
I saw the brown heath growing there.

It was scattered and stunted, and told me
That soon even that would be gone;
Its whispered, 'The grim walls enfold me;
I have bloomed in my last summer's sun.' . . .

The spirit that bent 'neath its power,
How it longed, how it burned to be free!
If I could have wept in that hour
Those tears had been heaven to me.

Well, well, the sad minutes are moving
Though loaded with trouble and pain;
And sometime the loved and the loving
Shall meet on the mountains again.

November 11, 1838

A little while, a little while,
The noisy crowd are barred away;
And I can sing and I can smile
A little while I've holyday!

Where wilt thou go, my harassed heart?
Full many a land invites thee now;
And places near and far apart
Have rest for thee, my weary brow.

There is a spot 'mid barren hills
Where winter howls and driving rain,
But if the dreary tempest chills
There is a light that warms again.

The house is old, the trees are bare
And moonless bends the misty dome
But what on earth is half so dear,
So longed for as the hearth of home?

The mute bird sitting on the stone,
The dank moss dripping from the wall,
The garden-walk with weeds o'ergrown,
I love them—how I love them all!

Shall I go there? or shall I seek
Another clime, another sky,
Where tongues familiar music speak
In accents dear to memory?

Yes, as I mused, the naked room,
The flickering firelight died away
And from the midst of cheerless gloom
I passed to bright, unclouded day—

A little and a lone green lane
That opened on a common wide;
A distant, dreamy, dim blue chain
Of mountains circling every side;

A heaven so clear, an earth so calm,
So sweet, so soft, so hushed an air
And, deepening still the dream-like charm,
Wild moor-sheep feeding everywhere—

That was the scene; I knew it well,
I knew the path-ways far and near
That winding o'er each billowy swell
Marked out the tracks of wandering deer.

Could I have lingered but an hour
It well had paid a week of toil,
But truth has banished fancy's power;
I hear my dungeon bars recoil—

Even as I stood with raptured eye
Absorbed in bliss so deep and dear
My hour of rest had fleeted by
And given me back to weary care.

December 4, 1838

[7]

How still, how happy! Those are words
That once would scarce agree together;
I loved the plashing of the surge,
The changing heaven, the breezy weather,

More than smooth seas and cloudless skies
And solemn, soothing, softened airs
That in the forest woke no sighs
And from the green spray shook no tears.

How still, how happy! Now I feel
Where silence dwells is sweeter far
Than laughing mirth's most joyous swell
However pure its raptures are.

Come, sit down on this sunny stone:
'Tis wintry light o'er flowerless moors—
But sit—for we are all alone
And clear expand heaven's breathless shores.

I could think in the withered grass
Spring's budding wreaths we might discern;
The violet's eye might shyly flash
And young leaves shoot among the fern.

It is but thought—full many a night
The snow shall clothe those hills afar
And storms shall add a drearier blight
And winds shall wage a wilder war,

Before the lark may herald in
Fresh foliage twined with blossoms fair
And summer days again begin
Their glory-haloed crown to wear.

41

Yet my heart loves December's smile
As much as July's golden beam;
Then let us sit and watch the while
The blue ice curdling on the stream.

December 7, 1838

[8]

TO THE BLUEBELL

Sacred watcher, wave thy bells!
Fair hill flower and woodland child!
Dear to me in deep green dells—
Dearest on the mountains wild.

Bluebell, even as all divine
I have seen my darling shine—
Bluebell, even as wan and frail
I have seen my darling fail—
Thou hast found a voice for me,
And soothing words are breathed by thee.

Thus they murmur, 'Summer's sun
Warms me till my life is done.
Would I rather choose to die
Under winter's ruthless sky?

'Glad I bloom and calm I fade;
Weeping twilight dews my bed;
Mourner, mourner, dry thy tears—
Sorrow comes with lengthened years!'

May 9, 1839

9

WRITTEN ON RETURNING TO THE
P. OF I. ON THE 10TH OF JANUARY, 1827

The busy day has hurried by,
And hearts greet kindred hearts once more;
And swift the evening hours should fly,
But—what turns every gleaming eye
So often to the door,

And then so quick away—and why
Does sudden silence chill the room,
And laughter sink into a sigh,
And merry words to whispers die,
And gladness change to gloom?

O we are listening for a sound
We know shall ne'er be heard again;
Sweet voices in the halls resound,
Fair forms, fond faces gather round,
But all in vain—in vain!

Their feet shall never waken more
The echoes in these galleries wide,
Nor dare the snow on the mountain's brow,
Nor skim the river's frozen flow,
Nor wander down its side.

They who have been our life—our soul—
Through summer-youth, from childhood's spring—
Who bound us in one vigorous whole
To stand 'gainst Tyranny's control
For ever triumphing—

43

Who bore the brunt of battle's fray:
The first to fight, the last to fall;
Whose mighty minds, with kindred ray,
Still led the van in Glory's way;
The idol chiefs of all—

They, they are gone! Not for a while
As golden suns at night decline
And even in death our grief beguile
Foretelling, with a rose-red smile,
How bright the morn will shine.

No; these dark towers are lone and lorn;
This very crowd is vacancy;
And we must watch and wait and mourn
And half look out for their return,
And think their forms we see;

And fancy music in our ear,
Such as their lips could only pour;
And think we feel their presence near,
And start to find they are not here,
And never shall be more!

June 14, 1839

'Well, some may hate, and some may scorn,
And some may quite forget thy name,
But my sad heart must ever mourn
Thy ruined hopes, thy blighted fame.'

'Twas thus I thought, an hour ago,
Even weeping o'er that wretch's woe.
One word turned back my gushing tears,
And lit my altered eye with sneers.

'Then bless the friendly dust,' I said,
'That hides thy unlamented head.
Vain as thou wert, and weak as vain,
The slave of falsehood, pride and pain,
My heart has nought akin to thine—
Thy soul is powerless over mine.'

But these were thoughts that vanished too—
Unwise, unholy, and untrue—
Do I despise the timid deer
Because his limbs are fleet with fear?

Or would I mock the wolf's death-howl
Because his form is gaunt and foul?
Or hear with joy the leveret's cry
Because it cannot bravely die?

No! Then above his memory
Let pity's heart as tender be:
Say, 'Earth lie lightly on that breast,
And, kind Heaven, grant that spirit rest!'

November 14, 1839

And like myself lone, wholly lone,
It sees the day's long sunshine glow;
And like myself it makes its moan
In unexhausted woe.

Give we the hills our equal prayer:
Earth's breezy hills and heaven's blue sea;
We ask for nothing further here
But our own hearts and liberty.

Ah! could my hand unlock its chain,
How gladly would I watch it soar,
And ne'er regret and ne'er complain
To see its shining eyes no more.

But let me think that if to-day
It pines in cold captivity,
To-morrow both shall soar away,
Eternally, entirely Free.

February 27, 1841

Riches I hold in light esteem
And Love I laugh to scorn
And lust of Fame was but a dream
That vanished with the morn—

And if I pray, the only prayer
That moves my lips for me
Is—'Leave the heart that now I bear
And give me liberty.'

Yes, as my swift days near their goal
'Tis all that I implore—
Through life and death, a chainless soul
With courage to endure!

March 1, 1841

[13]

Aye, there it is! It wakes to-night
Sweet thoughts that will not die
And feeling's fires flash all as bright
As in the years gone by!

And I can tell by thine altered cheek
And by thy kindled gaze
And by the words thou scarce dost speak,
How wildly fancy plays.

Yes, I could swear that glorious wind
Has swept the world aside,
Has dashed its memory from thy mind
Like foam-bells from the tide—

And thou art now a spirit pouring
Thy presence into all—
The essence of the Tempest's roaring
And of the Tempest's fall—

A universal influence
From Thine own influence free;
A principle of life, intense,
Lost to mortality.

Thus truly when that breast is cold
Thy prisoned soul shall rise,
The dungeon mingle with the mould—
The captive with the skies.

July 6, 1841

48

I see around me tombstones grey
Stretching their shadows far away.
Beneath the turf my footsteps tread
Lie low and lone the silent dead;
Beneath the turf, beneath the mould—
For ever dark, for ever cold,
And my eyes cannot hold the tears
That memory hoards from vanished years;
For Time and Death and Mortal pain
Give wounds that will not heal again.
Let me remember half the woe
I've seen and heard and felt below,
And Heaven itself, so pure and blest,
Could never give my spirit rest.
Sweet land of light! thy children fair
Know nought akin to our despair;
Nor have they felt, nor can they tell
What tenants haunt each mortal cell,
What gloomy guests we hold within—
Torments and madness, tears and sin!
Well, may they live in ecstasy
Their long eternity of joy;
At least we would not bring them down
With us to weep, with us to groan.
No—Earth would wish no other sphere
To taste her cup of sufferings drear;
She turns from Heaven a careless eye
And only mourns that *we* must die!
Ah mother, what shall comfort thee
In all this boundless misery?

49

To cheer our eager eyes a while
We see thee smile; how fondly smile!
But who reads not through that tender glow
Thy deep, unutterable woe?
Indeed no dazzilng land above
Can cheat thee of thy children's love.
We all, in life's departing shine,
Our last dear longings blend with thine;
And struggle still and strive to trace
With clouded gaze, thy darling face.
We would not leave our native home
For *any* world beyond the Tomb.
No—rather on thy kindly breast
Let us be laid in lasting rest;
Or waken but to share with thee
A mutual immortality.

July 17, 1841

15

M.G. FOR THE U.S. (UNIQUE SOCIETY)

'Twas yesterday, at early dawn,
I watched the falling snow;
A drearier scene on winter morn
Was never stretched below.

I could not see the mountains round,
But I knew by the wild wind's roar
How every drift, in their glens profound,
Was deepening ever more.

And then I thought of Ula's bowers
Beyond the southern sea;
Her tropic prairies bright with flowers
And rivers wandering free.

I thought of many a happy day
Spent in her Eden isle,
With my dear comrades, young and gay,
All scattered now so far away,
But not forgot the while!

Who that has breathed that heavenly air,
To northern climes would come,
To Gondal's mists and moorlands drear,
And sleet and frozen gloom?

Spring brings the swallow and the lark:
But what will winter bring?
Its twilight noons and evenings dark
To match the gifts of spring?

No! Look with me o'er that sullen main:
If thy spirit's eye can see,
There are brave ships floating back again
That no calm southern port could chain
From Gondal's stormy sea.

O how the hearts of the voyagers beat
To feel the frost-wind blow!
What flower in Ula's gardens sweet
Is worth one flake of snow?

The blast which almost rends their sail
Is welcome as a friend;
It brings them home, that thundering gale,
Home to their journey's end;

Home to our souls whose wearying sighs
Lament their absence drear,
And feel how bright even winter skies
Would shine if they were here!

December 19, 1843

16

MY COMFORTER

Well hast thou spoken—and yet not taught
A feeling strange or new;
Thou hast but raised a latent thought,
A cloud-closed beam of sunshine brought
To gleam in open view.

Deep down—concealed within my soul
That light lies hid from men,
Yet glows unquenched—though shadows roll,
Its gentle ray cannot control—
About the sullen den.

Was I not vexed, in these gloomy ways
To walk unlit so long?
Around me, wretches uttering praise,
Or howling o'er their hopeless days,
And each with Frenzy's tongue—

A Brotherhood of misery,
With smiles as sad as sighs;
Their madness daily maddening me,
And turning into agony
The Bliss before my eyes.

So stood I, in Heaven's glorious sun
And in the glare of Hell
My spirit drank a mingled tone
Of seraph's song and demon's moan—
What my soul bore my soul alone
Within its self may tell.

Like a soft air above a sea
Tossed by the tempest's stir—
A thaw-wind melting quietly
The snowdrift on some wintery lea:
No—what sweet thing can match with thee,
My thoughtful Comforter?

And yet a little longer speak,
Calm this resentful mood,
And while the savage heart grows meek,
For other token do not seek,
But let the tear upon my cheek
Evince my gratitude.

February 10, 1844

The linnet in the rocky dells,
The moor-lark in the air,
The bee among the heather-bells
That hide my lady fair:

The wild deer browse above her breast;
The wild birds raise their brood;
And they, her smiles of love caressed,
Have left her solitude!

I ween, that when the grave's dark wall
Did first her form retain,
They thought their hearts could ne'er recall
The light of joy again.

They thought the tide of grief would flow
Unchecked through future years,
But where is all their anguish now,
And where are all their tears?

Well, let them fight for Honour's breath,
Or Pleasure's shade pursue—
The Dweller in the land of Death
Is changed and careless too.

And if their eyes should watch and weep
Till sorrow's source were dry,
She would not, in her tranquil sleep,
Return a single sigh.

Blow, west wind, by the lonely mound,
And murmur, summer streams,
There is no need of other sound
To soothe my Lady's dreams.

May 1, 1844

TO IMAGINATION

When weary with the long day's care,
And earthly change from pain to pain,
And lost, and ready to despair,
Thy kind voice calls me back again—
O my true friend, I am not lone
While thou canst speak with such a tone!

So hopeless is the world without,
The world within I doubly prize;
Thy world where guile and hate and doubt
And cold suspicion never rise;
Where thou and I and Liberty
Have undisputed sovereignty.

What matters it that all around
Danger and grief and darkness lie,
If but within our bosom's bound
We hold a bright unsullied sky,
Warm with ten thousand mingled rays
Of suns that know no winter days?

Reason indeed may oft complain
For Nature's sad reality,
And tell the suffering heart how vain
Its cherished dreams must always be;
And Truth may rudely trample down
The flowers of Fancy newly blown.

But thou art ever there to bring
The hovering visions back and breathe

New glories o'er the blighted spring
And call a lovelier life from death,
And whisper with a voice divine
Of real worlds as bright as thine.

I trust not to thy phantom bliss,
Yet still in evening's quiet hour
With never-failing thankfulness
I welcome thee, benignant power,
Sure solacer of human cares
And brighter hope when hope despairs.

September 3, 1844

[19]

O thy bright eyes must answer now,
When Reason, with a scornful brow,
Is mocking at my overthrow;
O thy sweet tongue must plead for me
And tell why I have chosen thee!

Stern Reason is to judgement come
Arrayed in all her forms of gloom:
Wilt thou my advocate be dumb?
No, radiant angel, speak and say
Why I did cast the world away;

Why I have persevered to shun
The common paths that others run;
And on a strange road journeyed on
Heedless alike of Wealth and Power—
Of Glory's wreath and Pleasure's flower.

57

These once indeed seemed Beings divine,
And they perchance heard vows of mine
And saw my offerings on their shrine—
But, careless gifts are seldom prized,
And mine were worthily despised;

So with a ready heart I swore
To seek their altar-stone no more,
And gave my spirit to adore
Thee, ever present, phantom thing—
My slave, my comrade, and my King!

A slave because I rule thee still;
Incline thee to my changeful will
And make thy influence good or ill—
A comrade, for by day and night
Thou art my intimate delight—

My Darling Pain that wounds and sears
And wrings a blessing out from tears
By deadening me to real cares;
And yet, a king—though prudence well
Have taught thy subject to rebel.

And am I wrong to worship where
Faith cannot doubt nor Hope despair
Since my own soul can grant my prayer?
Speak, God of Visions, plead for me
And tell why I have chosen thee!

October 14, 1844

20

I.M. TO I.G.

'The winter wind is loud and wild;
Come close to me, my darling child!
Forsake thy books and mateless play,
And, while the night is closing grey,
We'll talk its pensive hours away—

'Iernë, round our sheltered hall,
November's blasts unheeded call;
Not one faint breath can enter here
Enough to wave my daughter's hair;

'And I am glad to watch the blaze
Glance from her eyes, with mimic rays;
To feel her cheek so softly pressed
In happy quiet on my breast;

'But, yet, even this tranquillity
Brings bitter, restless thoughts to me;
And, in the red fire's cheerful glow,
I think of deep glens, blocked with snow;

'I dream of moor, and misty hill,
Where evening gathers, dark and chill,
For, lone, among the mountains cold
Lie those that I have loved of old,
And my heart aches, in speechless pain,
Exhausted with repinings vain,
That I shall see them ne'er again!'

'Father, in early infancy,
When you were far beyond the sea,

Such thoughts were tyrants over me—
I often sat for hours together,
Through the long nights of angry weather,
Raised on my pillow, to descry
The dim moon struggling in the sky;
Or, with strained ear, to catch the shock
Of rock with wave, and wave with rock.
So would I fearful vigil keep,
And, all for listening, never sleep;
But this world's life has much to dread;
Not so, my father, with the Dead.

'O not for them should we despair;
The grave is drear, but they are not there:
Their dust is mingled with the sod;
Their happy souls are gone to God!
You told me this, and yet you sigh,
And murmur that your friends must die.
Ah, my dear father, tell me why?

'For, if your former words were true,
How useless would such sorrow be!
As wise to mourn the seed which grew
Unnoticed on its parent tree,

'Because it fell in fertile earth
And sprang up to a glorious birth—
Struck deep its roots, and lifted high
Its green boughs in the breezy sky!

'But I'll not fear—I will not weep
For those whose bodies lie asleep:
I know there is a blessed shore

Opening its ports for me and mine;
And, gazing Time's wide waters o'er,
I weary for that land divine,

'Where we were born—where you and I
Shall meet our dearest, when we die;
From suffering and corruption free,
Restored into the Deity.'

'Well hast thou spoken, sweet, trustful child!
And wiser than thy sire:
And coming tempests, raging wild,
Shall strengthen thy desire—
Thy fervent hope, through storm and foam,
Through wind and Ocean's roar,
To reach, at last, the eternal home—
The steadfast, changeless shore!'

November 6, 1844

21

R. ALCONA TO J. BRENZAIDA

Cold in the earth, and the deep snow piled above thee!
Far, far removed, cold in the dreary grave!
Have I forgot, my Only Love, to love thee,
Severed at last by Time's all-wearing wave?

Now, when alone, do my thoughts no longer hover
Over the mountains on Angora's shore;
Resting their wings where heath and fern-leaves cover
That noble heart for ever, ever more?

Cold in the earth, and fifteen wild Decembers
From those brown hills have melted into spring—
Faithful indeed is the spirit that remembers
After such years of change and suffering!

Sweet Love of youth, forgive if I forget thee
While the World's tide is bearing me along:
Sterner desires and darker hopes beset me,
Hopes which obscure but cannot do thee wrong.

No other Sun has lightened up my heaven;
No other Star has ever shone for me:
All my life's bliss from thy dear life was given—
All my life's bliss is in the grave with thee.

But when the days of golden dreams had perished
And even Despair was powerless to destroy,
Then did I learn how existence could be cherished,
Strengthened and fed without the aid of joy;

Then did I check the tears of useless passion,
Weaned my young soul from yearning after thine;
Sternly denied its burning wish to hasten
Down to that tomb already more than mine!

And even yet, I dare not let it languish,
Dare not indulge in Memory's rapturous pain;
Once drinking deep of that divinest anguish,
How could I seek the empty world again?

March 3, 1845

22

Ah! why, because the dazzling sun
Restored my earth to joy
Have you departed, every one,
And left a desert sky?

All through the night, your glorious eyes
Were gazing down in mine,
And with a full heart's thankful sighs
I blessed that watch divine!

I was at peace, and drank your beams
As they were life to me
And revelled in my changeful dreams
Like petrel on the sea.

Thought followed thought—star followed star
Through boundless regions on,
While one sweet influence, near and far,
Thrilled through and proved us one.

Why did the morning rise to break
So great, so pure a spell,
And scorch with fire the tranquil cheek
Where your cool radiance fell?

Blood-red he rose, and arrow-straight
His fierce beams struck my brow;
The soul of Nature sprang elate,
But mine sank sad and low!

My lids closed down—yet through their veil
I saw him blazing still;
And bathe in gold the misty dale,
And flash upon the hill.

I turned me to the pillow then
To call back Night, and see
Your worlds of solemn light, again
Throb with my heart and me!

It would not do—the pillow glowed
And glowed both roof and floor,
And birds sang loudly in the wood,
And fresh winds shook the door.

The curtains waved, the wakened flies
Were murmuring round my room,
Imprisoned there, till I should rise
And give them leave to roam.

O Stars and Dreams and Gentle Night;
O Night and Stars return!
And hide me from the hostile light
That does not warm, but burn—

That drains the blood of suffering men;
Drinks tears, instead of dew:
Let me sleep through his blinding reign,
And only wake with you!

April 14, 1845

23

A. E. AND R. C.

Heavy hangs the raindrop
From the burdened spray;
Heavy broods the damp mist
On uplands far away;

Heavy looms the dull sky,
Heavy rolls the sea—
And heavy beats the young heart
Beneath that lonely tree.

Never has a blue streak
Cleft the clouds since morn—
Never has his grim Fate
Smiled since he was born.

Frowning on the infant,
Shadowing childhood's joy,
Guardian angel knows not
That melancholy boy.

Day is passing swiftly
Its sad and sombre prime;
Youth is fast invading
Sterner manhood's time.

All the flowers are praying
For sun before they close,
And he prays too, unknowing,
That sunless human rose!

Blossoms, that the west wind
Has never wooed to blow,
Scentless are your petals,
Your dew as cold as snow.

Soul, where kindred kindness
No early promise woke,
Barren is your beauty
As weed upon the rock.

Wither, Brothers, wither,
You were vainly given—
Earth reserves no blessing
For the unblessed of Heaven!

May 28, 1845

Child of Delight! with sunbright hair,
And seablue, seadeep eyes;
Spirit of Bliss, what brings thee here,
Beneath these sullen skies?

Thou shouldest live in eternal spring,
Where endless day is never dim;
Why, seraph, has thy erring wing
Borne thee down to weep with him?

'Ah! not from heaven am I descended,
And I do not come to mingle tears;
But sweet is day, though with shadows blended;
And, though clouded, sweet are youthful years.

'I, the image of light and gladness,
Saw and pitied that mournful boy,
And I swore to take his gloomy sadness,
And give to him my beamy joy.

'Heavy and dark the night is closing;
Heavy and dark may its biding be:
Better for all from grief reposing,
And better for all who watch like me.

'Guardian angel, he lacks no longer;
Evil fortune he need not fear:
Fate is strong, but Love is stronger;
And more unsleeping than angel's care.'

1845

How beautiful the Earth is still
To thee—how full of Happiness;
How little fraught with real ill
Or shadowy phantoms of distress;

How Spring can bring thee glory yet
And Summer win thee to forget
December's sullen time!
Why dost thou hold the treasure fast
Of youth's delight, when youth is past
And thou art near thy prime?

When those who were thy own compeers,
Equal in fortunes and in years,
Have seen their morning melt in tears,
To dull unlovely day;
Blest, had they died unproved and young
Before their hearts were wildly wrung,
Poor slaves, subdued by passions strong,
A weak and helpless prey!

'Because, I hoped while they enjoyed,
And by fulfilment, hope destroyed—
As children hope, with trustful breast,
I waited Bliss and cherished Rest.

'A thoughtful Spirit taught me soon
That we must long till life be done;
That every phase of earthly joy
Will always fade and always cloy—

69

'This I foresaw, and would not chase
The fleeting treacheries,
But with firm foot and tranquil face
Held backward from the tempting race,
Gazed o'er the sands the waves efface
To the enduring seas—

'There cast my anchor of Desire
Deep in unknown Eternity;
Nor ever let my Spirit tire
With looking for *What is to be.*

'It is Hope's spell that glorifies
Like youth to my maturer eyes
All Nature's million mysteries—
The fearful and the fair—

'Hope soothes me in the griefs I know,
She lulls my pain for others' woe
And makes me strong to undergo
What I am born to bear.

'Glad comforter, will I not brave
Unawed the darkness of the grave?
Nay, smile to hear Death's billows rave,
My Guide, sustained by thee?
The more unjust seems present fate
The more my Spirit springs elate
Strong in thy strength, to anticipate
Rewarding Destiny!

June 2, 1845

Silent is the House—all are laid asleep;
One, alone, looks out o'er the snow wreaths deep;
Watching every cloud, dreading every breeze
That whirls the 'wildering drifts and bends the groaning trees.

Cheerful is the hearth, soft the matted floor;
Not one shivering gust creeps through pane or door;
The little lamp burns straight, its rays shoot strong and far;
I trim it well to be the Wanderer's guiding-star.

Frown, my haughty sire; chide, my angry dame;
Set your slaves to spy, threaten me with shame:
But neither sire nor dame, nor prying serf shall know
What angel nightly tracks that waste of winter snow.

What I love shall come like visitant of air,
Safe in secret power from lurking human snare;
Who loves me, no word of mine shall e'er betray,
Though for faith unstained my life must forfeit pay.

Burn, then, little lamp; glimmer straight and clear—
Hush! a rustling wing stirs, methinks, the air:
He for whom I wait, thus ever comes to me;
Strange Power! I trust thy might; trust thou my constancy.

October 9, 1845

JULIAN M. AND A. G. ROCHELLE

In the dungeon crypts idly did I stray,
Reckless of the lives wasting there away;
'Draw the ponderous bars; open, Warder stern!'
He dare not say me nay—the hinges harshly turn.

'Our guests are darkly lodged,' I whispered, gazing through
The vault whose grated eye showed heaven more grey
    than blue.
(This was when glad spring laughed in awaking pride.)
'Aye, darkly lodged enough!' returned my sullen guide.

Then, God forgive my youth, forgive my careless tongue!
I scoffed, as the chill chains on the damp flagstones rung;
'Confined in triple walls, art thou so much to fear,
That we must bind thee down and clench thy fetters here?'

The captive raised her face; it was as soft and mild
As sculptured marble saint or slumbering, unweaned child;
It was so soft and mild, it was so sweet and fair,
Pain could not trace a line nor grief a shadow there!

The captive raised her hand and pressed it to her brow:
'I have been struck,' she said, 'and I am suffering now;
Yet these are little worth, your bolts and irons strong;
And were they forged in steel they could not hold me long.'

Hoarse laughed the jailor grim: 'Shall I be won to hear;
Dost think, fond dreaming wretch, that *I* shall grant thy
    prayer?
Or, better still, wilt melt my master's heart with groans?
Ah, sooner might the sun thaw down these granite stones!

'My master's voice is low, his aspect bland and kind,
But hard as hardest flint the soul that lurks behind;
And I am rough and rude, yet not more rough to see
Than is the hidden ghost which has its home in me!'

About her lips there played a smile of almost scorn:
'My friend,' she gently said, 'you have not heard me mourn;
When you my parents' lives—*my* lost life, can restore,
Then may I weep and sue—but *never*, Friend, before!'

Her head sank on her hands; its fair curls swept the ground;
The dungeon seemed to swim in strange confusion round—
'Is she so near to death?' I murmured, half aloud,
And, kneeling, parted back the floating golden cloud . . .

She knew me and she sighed, 'Lord Julian, can it be,
Of all my playmates, you alone remember me?
Nay, start not at my words, unless you deem it shame
To own, from conquered foe, a once familiar name.

'I cannot wonder now at ought the world will do,
And insult and contempt I lightly brook from you,
Since those, who vowed away their souls to win my love,
Around this living grave like utter strangers move! . . .

'Yet, tell them, Julian, all, I am not doomed to wear
Year after year in gloom and desolate despair;
A messenger of Hope comes every night to me,
And offers, for short life, eternal liberty.

'He comes with western winds, with evening's
    wandering airs,
With that clear dusk of heaven that brings the thickest stars;
Winds take a pensive tone, and stars a tender fire,
And visions rise and change which kill me with desire—

'Desire for nothing known in my maturer years
When joy grew mad with awe at counting future tears;
When, if my spirit's sky was full of flashes warm,
I knew not whence they came, from sun or thunderstorm;

'But first a hush of peace, a soundless calm descends;
The struggle of distress and fierce impatience ends;
Mute music soothes my breast—unuttered harmony
That I could never dream till earth was lost to me.

'Then dawns the Invisible, the Unseen its truth reveals;
My outward sense is gone, my inward essence feels—
Its wings are almost free, its home, its harbour found;
Measuring the gulf it stoops and dares the final bound!

'Oh, dreadful is the check—intense the agony
When the ear begins to hear and the eye begins to see;
When the pulse begins to throb, the brain to think again,
The soul to feel the flesh and the flesh to feel the chain!

'Yet I would lose no sting, would wish no torture less;
The more that anguish racks the earlier it will bless;
And robed in fires of Hell, or bright with heavenly shine,
If it but herald Death, the vision is divine.' . . .

I heard, and yet heard not, the surly keeper growl;
I saw, yet did not see, the flagstone damp and foul.
The keeper, to and fro, paced by the bolted door
And shivered as he walked and, as he shivered, swore.

While my cheek glowed in flame, I marked that he did rave
Of air that froze his blood, and moisture like the grave—
'We have been two hours good!' he muttered peevishly;
Then, loosing off his belt the rusty dungeon key,

He said, 'You may be pleased, Lord Julian, still to stay,
But duty will not let me linger here all day;
If I might go, I'd leave this badge of mine with you,
Not doubting that you'd prove a jailor stern and true.' . . .

Nevertheless, Julian feels impelled to strike through the
prisoner's fetters and release her with the keys. He hides her in
his castle-home.

Through thirteen anxious weeks of terror-blent delight
I guarded her by day and guarded her by night,
While foes were prowling near and Death gazed greedily
And only Hope remained a faithful friend to me.

Then oft with taunting smile I heard my kindred tell
'How Julian loved his hearth and sheltering roof-tree well;
How the trumpet's voice might call, the battle-standard wave,
But Julian had no heart to fill a patriot's grave.'

And I, who am so quick to answer sneer with sneer;
So ready to condemn, to scorn, a coward's fear,
I held my peace like one whose conscience keeps him dumb,
And saw my kinsmen go—and lingered still at home.

Another hand than mine my rightful banner held
And gathered my renown on Freedom's crimson field;
Yet I had no desire the glorious prize to gain—
It needed braver nerve to face the world's disdain.

And by the patient strength that could that world defy,
By suffering, with calm mind, contempt and calumny;
By never-doubting love, unswerving constancy,
Rochelle, I earned at last an equal love from thee!

October 9, 1845

No coward soul is mine
No trembler in the world's storm-troubled sphere
I see Heaven's glories shine
And Faith shines equal arming me from Fear

O God within my breast
Almighty ever-present Deity
Life, that in me hast rest
As I Undying Life, have power in Thee

Vain are the thousand creeds
That move men's hearts, unutterably vain,
Worthless as withered weeds
Or idlest froth amid the boundless main

To waken doubt in one
Holding so fast by thy infinity
So surely anchored on
The steadfast rock of Immortality

With wide-embracing love
Thy spirit animates eternal years
Pervades and broods above,
Changes, sustains, dissolves, creates and rears

Though Earth and moon were gone
And suns and universes ceased to be
And thou wert left alone
Every Existence would exist in thee

There is not room for Death
Nor atom that his might could render void
Since thou art Being and Breath
And what thou art may never be destroyed.

January 2, 1846

[29]

Often rebuked, yet always back returning
  To those first feelings that were born with me,
And leaving busy chase of wealth and learning
  For idle dreams of things which cannot be:

To-day, I will seek not the shadowy region;
  Its unsustaining vastness waxes drear;
And visions rising, legion after legion,
  Bring the unreal world too strangely near.

I'll walk, but not in old heroic traces,
  And not in paths of high morality,
And not among the half-distinguished faces,
  The clouded forms of long-past history.

I'll walk where my own nature would be leading:
  It vexes me to choose another guide:
Where the gray flocks in ferny glens are feeding;
  Where the wild wind blows on the mountain side.

What have those lonely mountains worth revealing?
  More glory and more grief than I can tell:
The earth that wakes *one* human heart to feeling
  Can centre both the worlds of Heaven and Hell.

date unknown

is doubtless lost for when I came back
from Brussels I enquired. on all hands and
could hear nothing of him — as you did
early last year — Keeper and Flossy are well
also the canary acquired 4 years since
we are now all at home and likely to
be there some time — Branwell went
to Liverpool on ~~Monday~~ Thursday to stay a week
Tabby has just been teasing me to turn
as formerly to "pilloputate" — Anne and I
should have picked the black currants
if it had been fine and sunshiny. I must
hurry off now to my turning and ironing
I have plenty of work on hands and
writing and am altogether full of business
with best wishes for the whole
House till 1848 July 30th and as
much longer as may be I conclude

The final page of Emily's diary letter of July 30 1845 with her
drawing of herself and her dog Keeper. It was written on a tiny
piece of paper, folded to the size of a sixpence, found years after
her death in a little tin box about two inches long 'in which one
might keep pins or beads'.

THE DIARY LETTERS

November the 24 1834   Monday
Emily Jane Brontë
Anne Brontë

I fed Rainbow, Diamond Snowflake Jasper pheasent (alias). This morning Branwell went down to Mr Drivers and brought news that Sir Robert Peel was going to be invited to stand for Leeds. Anne and I have been peeling Apples for Charlotte to make an apple pudding and for Aunts nuts and apples. Charlotte said she made puddings perfectly and she was of a quick but limited intellect. Taby said just now Come Anne pilloputate (i.e. pill a potato). Aunt has come into the kitchen just now and said where are your feet Anne. Anne answered On the floor Aunt. Papa opened the parlour door and gave Branwell a letter saying here Branwell read this and show it to your Aunt and Charlotte —The Gondals are discovering the interior of Gaaldine. Sally Mosley is washing in the back-kitchin.

It is past Twelve o'clock. Anne and I have not tidied ourselves, done our bed work or done our lessons and we want to go out to play. We are going to have for Dinner Boiled Beef Turnips, potatoes and applepudding. The kitchin is in a very untidy state. Anne and I have not done our music exercise which consists of b major. Taby said on my putting a pen in her face Ya pitter pottering there instead of pilling a potate. I answered O Dear, O Dear, O Dear I will directly. With that I get up, take a knife and begin pilling (finished pilling the potatoes). Papa going to walk. Mr Sunderland expected.

Anne and I say I wonder what we shall be like and what we shall be and where we shall be if all goes on well in the year 1874— in which year I shall be in my 54th year, Anne will be going in her 55th year, Branwell will be going in his 58th year. And Charlotte in her 59th year. Hoping we shall all be well at that time we close our paper.

Emily and Anne
November the 24 1834

Monday evening June 26 1837

A bit past 4 o'clock, Charlotte working in Aunt's room, Branwell reading Eugene Aram to her—Anne and I writing in the drawing room—Anne a poem beginning "fair was the evening and brightly the sun"—I Agustus-Almedas life 1st v. 1–4th page from the last. A fine rather coolish thin grey cloudy but sunny day. Aunt working in the little room. Papa—gone out. Tabby in the Kitchin [sic]—the Emperors and Empresses of Gondal and Gaaldine preparing to depart from Gaaldine to Gondal to prepare for the coronation which will be on the 12th of July. Queen Vittiora [sic] ascended the throne this month. Northangerland in Monceys Isle—Zamorna at Eversham. All tight and right in which condition it is to be hoped we shall all be on this day 4 years at which time Charlotte will be 25 and 2 months—Branwell just 24 it being his birthday—myself 22 and 10 months and a peice [sic] Anne 21 and nearly a half. I wonder where we shall be and how we shall be and what kind of a day it will be then. Let us hope for the best—

Emily Jane Brontë—Anne Brontë

A Paper to be opened
when Anne is
25 years old
or my next birthday after—
if
—all be well—
Emily Jane Brontë   July the 30th 1841

It is Friday evening—near 9 o'clock—wild rainy weather. I am seated in the dining room after having just concluded tidying our desk-boxes—writing this document. Papa is in the parlour. Aunt upstairs in her room. She has been reading Blackwood's Magazine to papa. Victoria and Adelaide are ensconced in the peat-house. Keeper is in the kitchen. Hero in his cage. We are all stout and hearty as I hope is the case with Charlotte, Branwell, and Anne, of whom the first is at John White Esq, Upperwood House, Rawdon. The second is at Luddenden Foot and the third's I believe at Scarborough—inditing perhaps, a paper corresponding to this.

A scheme is at present in agitation for setting us up in A School of our own; as yet nothing is determined but I hope and trust it may go on and prosper and answer our highest expectations. This day 4-years I wonder whether we shall still be dragging on in our present condition or established to our hearts' content. Time will show—

I guess that at the time appointed for the opening of this paper we, i.e. Charlotte, Anne and I—shall be all merrily seated in our own sitting-room in some pleasant and flourishing seminary, having just gathered in for the midsummer holidays. Our debts will be paid off and we shall have cash in hand to a considerable amount. Papa, Aunt and Branwell will either have been, or be coming to visit us. It will be a fine warm evening—very different from this bleak lookout. Anne and I will perchance slip out into the garden for a few minutes to piruse [*sic*] our papers. I hope either this or something better will be the case.

The Gondalians are at present in a threatening state but there is no open rupture as yet—all the princes and princesses of the royaltys are at the Palace of Instruction. I have a good many books on hand, but I am sorry to say that as usual I make small progress with any. However, I have just made a new regularity paper! and I will—Verb Sap—to do great things. And now I close, sending from far an exhortation of courage. Courage! to exiled and harrassed [*sic*] Anne & wishing she was here.

July the 30th, A.D. 1841

This is Emily's birthday. She has now completed her 23rd year, and is, I believe, at home. Charlotte is a governess in the family of Mr White. Branwell is a clerk in the railroad station at Luddenden Foot, and I am a governess in the family of Mr Robinson. I dislike the situation and wish to change it for another. I am now at Scarborough. My pupils are gone to bed and I am hastening to finish this before I follow them.

We are thinking of setting up a school of our own, but nothing definite is settled about it yet, and we do not know whether we shall be able to or not. I hope we shall. And I wonder what will be our condition and how or where we shall all be on this day four years hence; at which time, if all be well, I shall be 25 years and 6 months old, Emily will be 27 years old, Branwell 28 years and 1 month, and Charlotte 29 years and a quarter. We are now all separate and not likely to meet again for many a weary week, but we are none of us ill that I know of and all are doing something for our own livelihood except Emily, who, however, is as busy as any of us, and in reality earns her food and raiment as much as we do.

> How little know we what we are
> How less what we may be!

Four years ago I was at school. Since then I have been a governess at Blake Hall, left it, come to Thorp Green, and seen the sea and York Minister. Emily has been a teacher at Miss Patchet's school, and left it. Charlotte has left Miss Wooler's, been a governess at Mrs Sidgwick's, left her, and gone to Mrs White's. Branwell has given up painting, been a tutor in Cumberland, left it, and become a clerk on the railroad. Tabby has left us, Martha Brown has come in her place. We have got Keeper, got a sweet little cat and lost it, and also got a hawk. Got a wild goose which has flown away, and three tame ones, one of which has been killed. All these diversities, with many others, are things we did not expect or foresee in the July of 1837. What will the next four years bring forth? Providence only knows. But we ourselves have sustained very little alteration since that time. I have the same faults that I had then, only I have more wisdom and experience, and a little more self-possession than I then enjoyed. How will it be when we open this paper and the one Emily has written? I wonder whether the Gondaliand [sic] will still be flourishing, and what will be their condition. I am now engaged in writing the fourth volume of Solala Vernon's Life.

For some time I have looked upon 25 as a sort of era in my existence. It may prove a true presentiment, or it may be only a superstitious fancy; the latter seems most likely, but time will show.

Anne Brontë

Haworth, Thursday, July 30th, 1845
My birthday—showery, breezy, cool. I am twenty-seven years old to-day. This morning Anne and I opened the papers we wrote four years since, on my twenty-third birthday. This paper we

intend, if all be well, to open on my thirtieth—three years hence, in 1848. Since the 1841 paper the following events have taken place. Our school scheme has been abandoned, and instead Charlotte and I went to Brussels on the 8th of February 1842.

Branwell left his place at Luddenden Foot. C. and I returned from Brussels, November 8th 1842, in consequence of aunt's death.

Branwell went to Thorp Green as a tutor, where Anne still continued, January 1843.

Charlotte returned to Brussels the same month, and, after staying a year, came back again on New Year's Day 1844.

Anne left her situation at Thorp Green of her own accord, June 1845.

Anne and I went our first long journey by ourselves together, leaving home on the 30th of June, Monday, sleeping at York, returning to Keighley Tuesday evening, sleeping there and walking home on Wednesday morning. Though the weather was broken we enjoyed ourselves very much, except during a few hours at Bradford. And during our excursion we were, Ronald Macalgin, Henry Angora, Juliet Angusteena, Rosabella Esmalden, Ella and Julian Egremont, Catharine Navarre, and Cordelia Fitzaphnold, escaping from the palaces of instruction to join the Royalists who are hard driven at present by the victorious Republicans. The Gondals still flourish bright as ever. I am at present writing a work on the First Wars—Anne has been writing some articles on this and a book by Henry Sophona. We intend sticking firm by the rascals as long as they delight us which I am glad to say they do at present. I should have mentioned that last summer the School Scheme was revived in full vigour. We had prospectuses printed, despatched letters to all acquaintances imparting our plans and did our little all—but it was found no go —now I don't desire a school at all and none of us have any great longing for it. We have cash enough for our present wants with a prospect of accumulation. We are all in decent health, only that papa has a complaint in his eyes and with the exception of B. who I hope will be better and do better, hereafter. I am quite contented for myself—not as idle as formerly, altogether as hearty and having learnt to make the most of the present and hope for the future with less fidgetness that I cannot do all I wish—seldom or ever troubled with nothing to do and merely desiring that every body could be as comfortable as myself and as undesponding and then we should have a very tolerable world of it.

By mistake I find we have opened the paper on the 31st instead of the 30th. Yesterday was much such a day as this but the morning was divine.

Tabby who was gone in our last paper is come back and has lived with us two years and a half and is in good health. Martha who also departed is here too. We have got Flossy, got and lost Tiger, lost the hawk Hero which with the geese was given away, and is doubtless dead, for when I came back from Brussels I inquired on all hands and could hear nothing of him. Tiger died early last year. Keeper and Flossy are well, also the canary acquired four years since. We are now all at home, and likely to be there some time. Branwell went to Liverpool on Tuesday to stay a week. Tabby has just been teasing me to turn as formerly to 'pilloputate.' Anne and I should have picked the black currants if it had been fine and sunshiny. I must hurry off now to my turning and ironing. I have plenty of work on hands, and writing, and am altogether full of business. With best wishes for the whole house till 1848, July 30th, and as much longer as may be,—I conclude. Emily Brontë.

Thursday, July the 31st, 1845. Yesterday was Emily's birthday, and the time when we should have opened our 1845 paper, but by mistake we opened it to-day instead. How many things have happened since it was written—some pleasant, some far otherwise. Yet I was then at Thorp Green, and now I am only just escaped from it. I was wishing to leave it then, and if I had known that I had four years longer to stay how wretched I should have been; but during my stay I have had some very unpleasant and undreamt-of experiences of human nature. Others have seen more changes. Charlotte has left Mr White's and been twice to Brussels, where she stayed each time nearly a year. Emily has been there too, and stayed nearly a year. Branwell has left Luddenden Foot, and been a tutor at Thorp Green, and had much tribulation and ill health. He was very ill on Thursday, but he went with John Brown to Liverpool, where he now is, I suppose; and we hope he will be better and do better in future. This is a dismal, cloudy, wet evening. We have had so far a very cold wet summer. Charlotte has lately been to Hathersage, in Derbyshire, on a visit of three weeks to Ellen Nussey. She is now sitting sewing in the dining-room. Emily is ironing upstairs. I am sitting in the dining-room in the rocking-chair before the fire with my feet on the fender. Papa is in the parlour. Tabby and Martha are, I think, in the kitchen. Keeper and Flossy are, I do not know where. Little Dick is hopping in his cage. When the last paper was written we were thinking of setting up a school. The scheme has been dropt, and long after taken up again and dropt again because we could not get pupils. Charlotte is thinking about getting another situation. She wishes to go to Paris. Will she go? She has let Flossy in, by-the-by, and he is now lying on the sofa. Emily is engaged in writing the Emperor Julius's life. She has read some of it, and I want very much to hear the rest. She is writing some poetry, too. I wonder what it is about? I have begun the third volume of Passages in the Life of an Individual. I wish I had finished it. This afternoon I began to set about making my grey figured silk frock that was dyed at Keighley. What sort of a hand shall I make of it? E. and I have a great deal of work to do. When shall we sensibly diminish it? I want to get a habit of early rising. Shall I succeed? We have not yet finished our Gondal Chronicles that we began three years and a half ago. When will they be done? The Gondals are at present in a sad state. The Republicans are uppermost, but the Royalists are not quite overcome. The young sovereigns, with their brothers and sisters, are still at the Palace of Instruction. The Unique Society, above half a year ago, were wrecked on a desert island as they were returning from Gaul. They are still there, but we have not played at them much yet. The Gondals in general are not in first-rate playing condition. Will they improve? I wonder how we shall all be and where and how situated on the thirtieth of July 1848, when, if we are all alive, Emily will be just 30. I shall be in my 29th year, Charlotte in her 33rd, and Branwell in his 32nd; and what changes shall we have seen and known; and shall we be much changed ourselves? I hope not, for the worse at least. I for my part cannot well be flatter or older in mind than I am now. Hoping for the best, I conclude.   Anne Brontë

NOTES

The main references are to *Poems* by Currer, Ellis and
Acton Bell (Aylott and Jones, 1846); to the selection of
poems in *Wuthering Heights and Agnes Grey* by Ellis and
Acton Bell, 'a new edition with a Biographical Notice of
the Authors, a selection from their literary remains, and a
Preface by Currer Bell' (Smith, Elder and Company,
1850); and to *The Complete Poems of Emily Jane Brontë*
edited from the manuscripts by C. W. Hatfield (Columbia
University Press, 1941).

1. 1836 was the year when Emily began to date and collect her poems.
   She did not include this in either of the fair-copy notebooks that
   Charlotte found in 1845, but the manuscript exists: you can see it
   at Haworth. It is an intensely exciting poem, owing something
   certainly to Scott, yet entirely personal in its sense of release, of a
   human creature joining in all that is freest and wildest in elemental
   nature. Emily had in fact left a 'drear dongeon' the year before—
   her three months at Roe Head. We know also that in two days'
   time, on December 15, Charlotte and Anne were expected home
   from school.

2. This poem is not in either of the notebooks. The manuscript,
   probably sold early in the century, has disappeared; Clement
   Shorter's copy is still the only source. It has no date; Hatfield
   places it among the early poems, and lines 15 and 16 certainly
   suggest this. The ecstatic yet gentle mood, both of the poet and of
   the moor itself (seen, unusually, on a tranquil, moonlit, warm
   spring night) also suggests the younger Emily, still in a time of
   hope and promise.

3. A manuscript fragment not copied into either of the notebooks.
   Apart from the curiously insistent effect of the word arrangement
   wind, rain, rain, wind, and the rhyming echoes of *mind* and *again,*
   the last two lines have a separate importance of their own. Land-
   scapes, events and legends stay alive in the mind—more power-
   fully, even for a Brontë, than if they were tangibly present.

86

4. Again, only Shorter's transcript (undated) can be found, but it is probably an early Gondal piece. Gondal's halls (like those in poems of Byron and Scott) were often echoing to the music of the harp. Music is almost always linked with memory (another powerful aspect of imagination) in Emily's poems. Of all the family, she was the most musically gifted, though all were taught, by visiting masters, from 1832 onwards. The piano was the instrument, though; there were no stringed instruments in the Parsonage. You may remember the passage in *Jane Eyre*, when Jane plays for Mr Rochester. He finds her performance only passable, but greatly admires her paintings and drawings! This seems to have been the accepted family rating; Charlotte shone as artist rather than as musician. The reverse held with Emily.

5. From the non-Gondal notebook; it was probably written or drafted while Emily was unhappily teaching at Law Hill near Halifax. Although she listed it herself as a 'personal' poem, and it is clearly this, it also shows how closely the Gondal world and the Haworth world were interlinked in Emily's imagination. A raging autumn storm (seen and heard from the imprisoning walls of a stranger's house) recalls some moment of the Gondal legend (see verse 2); within that fancy, certain 'wild words of an ancient song' take her out of the dark November exile to her own moorlands in the brightness of the spring. Not one of her poems suggests more ecstatically the loveliness of the moor in early summer. But there are memorable parallel passages in *Wuthering Heights*.

6. From the non-Gondal notebook, and very similar in mood to the previous poem, written three weeks earlier. But it is more precise in every way—a valuable key in its autobiographical detail. The detested Law Hill background (the 'dungeon bars' of the closing lines) with its 'noisy crowd' of schoolgirls, can hardly be mistaken. In this rare hour of freedom—freedom, above all, for her imagination—where, she asks, shall she send her thoughts? To Haworth ('There is a spot' mid barren hills')? or to Gondal ('Another clime, another sky')? Charlotte included the poem in the 1850 volume but left out the sixth verse. It needed, no doubt, too much explaining! Gondal and Angria were, to their authors, intensely private and remained so till long after all the Brontë deaths. Remember that, in the volume of 1846, Emily removed all Gondal names and references from her poems.

7. From the non-Gondal notebook. Contrast the deliberately patient mood (the first three verses are a fair summary of the whole) with

that of poem (1). It was not the first nor the only time that Emily would write of her love for the austere and flowerless winter of the moor, but the last line adds something new and arresting to the picture.

8. From the Gondal notebook—and clearly it hints at some lost story. But it can also remind us (as would, later, so many passages in *Wuthering Heights*) that the bluebell (or harebell) is essentially Emily Brontë's flower of the moorland summer, as the heather stands for the darker months of the year. This poem also exists in an early manuscript now in the British Museum. It is one of the few we have in Emily's ordinary handwriting, not in the more familiar Brontëan print-like script.

9. From the Gondal notebook—and it does offer some background clues to the lost saga. The P. of I. was the Palace of Instruction, a kind of aristocratic boarding school. (See the diary letter on p. 81.) The exact dating of the episode ('10th of January, 1827') is entirely characteristic of Emily's manner; we can see in *Wuthering Heights* (as well as in the birthday notes) how explicit she always was about ages and passages of time. Gondal dates, whenever they are given, go back to 1820s, when the 'secret plays' were first initiated—the years, too, of Emily's happy early childhood. Note that, in Gondal, Emily did not avoid the crowds that she shunned in daily life. The opening verses—verse 4 in particular —give a rare picture (rare for Emily, that is) of young people happily congregating together after school, talking, dancing, skating on the frozen river, wandering by its side. The great halls, 'dark towers', 'galleries wide' are typical of the mediaeval-romantic Gondal scene; there are plenty of these in Byron and Scott. Does the last verse hint, perhaps, at the two lost sisters, Maria and Elizabeth? Family legend, working on flashes of memory, may well have kept them alive in Emily's mind.

10. Surprisingly—for it seems to relate to some lost story—this is from the personal (non-Gondal) notebook. Though earlier biographers have claimed that its subject was Branwell, that can hardly be so; he did not die until the autumn of 1848. In November 1839, when Emily was 21 and Branwell 22, he was still a busy (if somewhat feverish and restless) member of the family; still enlivening company if unable to settle to any job for long. Even when Emily let this be published in the *Poems* of 1846 (with the enigmatic title 'Stanzas To—') Branwell still had a year and a half to live. At the

same time, it could well have expressed Emily's attitude to her brother's life and death.

11. Not in either of the notebooks, but the manuscript still exists, on a separate sheet (now in the Berg collection, New York Public Library). In the caged wild bird of the poem, enduring alone its endless hours of 'unexhausted woe', Emily sees an image of her own spirit, always threatened by restraint. There was enough in Victorian life whenever she entered it (as she had done as school-girl and school-teacher) to make her feel as imprisoned as the bird.

12. From the non-Gondal notebook. In the *Poems* of 1846 it was given the title 'The Old Stoic'. It contains the same thought as the caged bird poem, written a few days earlier. The ending words— 'With courage to endure'—were, very fittingly, chosen from all the Brontë writings to inscribe on their memorial tablet in Westminster Abbey.

13. From the non-Gondal notebook. It was first printed in the 1850 volume (with an additional verse by Charlotte). But far better than the unnecessary verse is Charlotte's inspired note: 'In these stanzas a louder gale has roused the sleeper on her pillow: the wakened soul struggles to blend with the storm by which it is swayed.' It is a strange and thrilling poem, nearer in feeling to Shelley than to any other poet in the language. The central verses memorably show how, in certain heightened conditions of nature, Emily's spirit or 'genius' (in the larger sense) seems to be carried away in a kind of ecstasy, perhaps to become part of the phenomenon itself. For the same experience see the poems on p. 33, p. 24, and others.

14. From the non-Gondal notebook. (The diary letters written a fortnight later show the general Brontëan situation at this time.) For all its unpromising look, this is an important and deeply interesting poem, containing what must be the plainest statement ever made by Emily about life on earth and life in the hereafter. No orthodox heaven, she declares, could hold the complexities of the human who has battled through the trials of the human world. Nor could the angels, heaven's 'children fair', know of the painful thoughts of mortal men. Earth, so closely identified with Nature, is too dear to lose. Here Emily voices this unconditionally. Better to have lasting rest in the earth—or, by becoming part of Nature (wind, leaf, earth, rain), to share in its non-human immortality.

Many passages in *Wuthering Heights* seem to be pre-figured by this poem—most notably the familiar one which ends the novel, when the narrator goes to look at the three headstones on the moor—Edgar's, Cathy's and Heathcliff's:

I lingered round them under that benign sky, watched the moths fluttering among the heath and harebells, listened to the soft wind breathing through the grass, and wondered how any one could ever imagine unquiet slumbers for the sleepers in that quiet earth.

15. From the Gondal notebook. Mr Nicholls, who made a copy, gave it the very reasonable title *North and South*. Though not a major poem, it is a haunting one in its way; the idea behind it is essential in Emily's thought—that, for all the heavenly mildness of the flower-bright South (as she puts it here), it cannot match the intense appeal of dark wild Gondal, with its 'glens profound', its 'moorlands drear', its 'sleet and frozen gloom'—the image, in fact, of her own loved Yorkshire scene. 'Home', 'journey's end' stood, of course, not only for Haworth but for the freedom of mind that went with it. Though Emily had now come home to stay, yet— even a year after leaving Brussels—the anguish of exile and excitement of return seem to be as sharply felt as ever. U.S. stands for Unique Society. See Anne's birthday note on p. 85.

16. From the non-Gondal notebook, and printed first in the 1846 *Poems*. It is a mysterious but rewarding poem, belonging in theme with those major personal works of her final writing year: poems (18), (19) and (25). Who, or what, is the Comforter? Is it the creative imagination, which always sustained her against darkness and despair? In (25) (see the final verse) the word is used again for something benignant and light-bringing. But compare the 'Darling Pain that wounds and sears' in (19). *My Comforter* certainly affirms once again the strength of Emily's inner resource; the triumphant and lyrical stoicism that seems peculiar to herself. It may seem odd that she was prepared to let such uniquely personal poems as this be printed in her lifetime. But Gondal was, for her, the secret that most needed cherishing and protecting.

17. From the Gondal notebook. Although there is a strange implicit tale, we are likely to notice first the scene, the heather-bells and Brontëan moorland creatures. Nature endures (the poem is saying),

indifferent to passing human grief. The departed human, too, the 'Dweller in the land of Death', now herself in the stream of elemental nature again, shares this indifference. The last two verses suggest once again the final passage of *Wuthering Heights*.

18. From the non-Gondal notebook, and one of the group of important personal poems of Emily's final years. After her return from Brussels in November 1842 (she was then 24), it was accepted at last that she should stay at home and follow her own way of life. From this time until the autumn of 1845 she was to write nearly all her outstanding poems; thereafter, as we know, the notebooks were 'discovered'. Here, she writes 'So hopeless is the world without/ The world within I doubly prize.' In that world within, imagination, liberty and the human spirit share equal rule—perhaps are all aspects of a single power. And yet, to the clear-sighted stoic, even imagination, a true, benignant shining friend, a 'brighter hope when hope despairs' must not be leaned on entirely.

19. From the non-Gondal notebook. One of Emily Brontë's major personal poems, it recalls the previous poem, written a few weeks earlier, but the thought is more complex and searching. As the last verse reveals, the spirit addressed is the God of Visions— Imagination, surely, by another name. Its gift, to those who truly possess it, is so supreme an independence and power that it is not hard to see why she voices her own allegiance in the form of a query in the final verse. Charlotte, an independent of another sort, seems to have had no theological doubts when she included this in the *Poems* of 1846.

20. From the Gondal notebook; it was still a solace to return to that wild country. This poem, with its deeply romantic, Scott-like echoes, has plenty of haunting lines. 'Iernë, round our sheltered hall/November's gusts unheeded call' is the kind of opening that lures one to read on. Through the father and daughter Emily looks at her own ideas on death and the hereafter. But the final lines, spoken by the father, are more in key with her own views than are the 'trustful' assurances of the child. Here, by the way, is one of a number of instances in which Emily sees eternity in the image of an ocean. In the 1846 volume the poem was given the title *Faith and Despondency*.

21. From the Gondal notebook; the striking opening and the line about the 'fifteen wild Decembers' have made it, through the

anthologies, one of the best-known of Emily Brontë's poems. This, of course, was the kind of material seized on by early biographers who, knowing nothing of Gondal (and certainly ignoring the ways in which writers work), determinedly saw it as a piece of personal history. Fifteen winters earlier, incidentally, Emily would not yet have been twelve years old. Nevertheless the two worlds are always interlinked, as we continually see in the poems. In the 1846 *Poems* it was given the title *Remembrance*.

22. From the non-Gondal notebook; first published (with the title *Stars*) in the 1846 *Poems*. It seems to describe, more than most, an immediate personal experience (see verses 8, 9, 10). Though Keats, Shelley, Byron, Coleridge and others of the great Romantic tide a generation earlier had all written memorable night-pieces, Emily's compelling tribute to the night is very much more than an echo of a fashionable mood. Certainly, she *could* suggest the rapture of bright summer daylight on the moors (in *Loud without,* for instance, and in many parts of *Wuthering Heights*). But night was always the time that freed her mind for visionary journeyings (see p. 73, last verse, p. 24 and others). Verse 4: again, an expression of the place of the human spirit (or of Emily Brontë's spirit) in the eternities of nature. Perhaps her greatest gift as a poet—one that she shared with the seventeenth-century Metaphysicals—is her ability to put into words a vast idea easily, briefly and with dazzling clarity.

23. Both poems, which are really meant to be taken together, are from
& the Gondal notebook, where the title *The Two Children* is written
24. (by Charlotte?) over the original heading. Whether or no Emily had started *Wuthering Heights* at this time (probably not) it was certainly in her mind; and these two poems are a clear pre-working of the novel's double theme of fair, loved girl and sullen, dark neglected boy—first, Cathy and Heathcliff, then the younger Catherine and Hareton. Both poems show how intrinsically, for Emily, Nature and human life were allied; see in the second, how exactly the bleak, boding, rain-like beat of the metre carries the thought. But as for what the enigmatic initials stand for in the title—the answer to that is lost with the lost Gondal stories.

25. From the non-Gondal notebook. It was included in the 1846 *Poems*, with the not very good title *Anticipation*. It is a stoical poem (Emily tells of rejecting the immediate gifts of the world), yet of rare poetic excitement. Reading, especially, the ten lines from 'This I foresaw' (which suggest the almost audacious reach of

Emily's imagination), and the final quatrain, we can understand why Charlotte wrote on the manuscript: 'Never was better stuff penned'.

26. From the Gondal notebook; the first three verses are, in fact, the opening of the long poem that follows. But in print, from its first appearance in the 1850 volume (with two extra verses, 4 and 5, added by Charlotte, and *The Visionary* as its title) and in countless anthologies since then, it has had a separate life of its own. Charlotte's addition however—good as it is—does alter any likely interpretation of the Wanderer. Who is speaking? Julian? Emily herself? What is the angel visitant, 'safe in secret power'? Rochelle? Her ghostly spirit? Emily's visionary Genius? This is a poem whose magic works for the reader by personal impact—for logic won't solve the enigma. Note how verse 1 forecasts in miniature the opening scene of *Wuthering Heights*. Note too how verse 3 shows that—even when Emily had advanced into the most searching regions of original thought, and was so near to the writing of her novel—she was still susceptible to the romantic mediaevalism which would run through nineteenth-century poetry, from Scott and Keats to the Pre-Raphaelites and Tennyson.

27. From the Gondal notebook—and probably the last poem that Emily was to write before the 'discovery'. A part of the very long whole was printed first in the 1846 *Poems* (the first eleven verses and then the seven magical verses beginning 'Yet, tell them, Julian, all')—one of the most extraordinary records in English poetry of the pains and ecstacies of a visionary experience. But apart from the 'Silent is the House' opening (first printed 1850: see note above) the rest remained unknown for nearly a century. This remainder is not so important. More important is the fact that here is the outstanding example of a Gondal daydream moving without a break into a passage of great writing which is also a unique personal statement. (The same phenomenon happens, of course, in any Shakespeare play.) Much could be said and little need be said about both the inner and outer poems; they are not outwardly obscure, and you gather as much as you bring. But if only one poem by Emily Bronte were to survive it would lie between this (*in toto*, for the great passage does not lose by the strangely moving Gondal narrative that encloses it) and *No coward soul is mine*. The word 'playmate' (verse 10) is touching and interesting. In Emily's Gondal, as in Emily's novel, the boy-girl camaraderie of the young might turn into a more passionate adult

relationship; but there is no trace of the feminine inequality that held in the early-Victorian outer world. George Meredith declared that, without equality of opponents, no true comedy was possible; the same thing holds, as Emily Brontë brilliantly shows, of tragedy. Incidentally, anyone doubting the range of her technical skill should look to see what astonishing effects are rendered in this poem by the alexandrine.

28. The best known and the greatest single poem by Emily Brontë, this is also the final entry in the personal notebook—though Charlotte's statement in the 1850 selection, that these were 'the last lines my sister ever wrote', is incorrect. There was an even later Gondal piece (see p. 18). We can only guess why it was not in the 1846 *Poems*, where Emily allowed the most revealing personal works to appear. Though written after the 'discovery' (and probably in mid-course of *Wuthering Heights*) it would still have been in time. But it fittingly stands at the end (or almost the end) of her poetry with its triumphant assurance, its sense of having passed the last stages of doubt and conflict. The manuscript has, unusually, no punctuation at the ends of the verses, as if the thought were too urgent for pause. This has made it possible for readers to isolate phrases (such as 'Vain are the thousand creeds . . .') that could seem to support any degree of theological belief or non-belief. But even when carefully read, without bias, the poem can vary its interpretations with the reader. Compare, for instance, the comments in two recent and interesting critical studies: *Emily Brontë* by Muriel Spark and Derek Stanford and *Emily Brontë* by John Hewish. Both these books are recommended (Hewish is also useful for current data on location of MSS. and such)—though for the full biographical treatment the studies by W. Gérin are unsurpassed. Stanford (who aptly describes the poem as 'private and subjective experience intellectualised to the highest degree, but still retaining the original colours of the mind which made it its own') declares that, after the seventeenth century, there is no religious poem in the English language to match it until the coming of Gerard Manley Hopkins. Hewish, who rates it no less highly, looks, rather, back to Shelley, especially to *Adonais*. A passage from the philosopher Herder, he suggests, exactly sums up the meaning: 'The power that thinks and works in me is in its nature as eternal as that which holds together the sun and stars'. Verses 2, 5 and 6 with their familiar audacious assertion of Emily's spiritual independence and of her particular conception of immortality are, when read in

this light, consistent with the thought in the great speculative poems that precede this masterwork.

29. A mystery hangs about this undated poem. It first appeared in the 1850 volume; but it is the only one among the 19 poems in that book for which no manuscript can be found. This has made some earlier editors suggest that Charlotte wrote it, but no one who has studied Emily's work seriously accepts this now. Charlotte may have added or altered an occasional word or line; she often did this—but in style and thought it could come from no other hand than Emily's. When was it written? It has all the air of being a later poem—apart from the fact that an early one of this quality would surely have been copied into the personal notebook. As it stands it is probably the most direct self-portrait we have of Emily Brontë. It reflects her solitary, stubborn, self-sufficient resistance to damaging outside stresses. It shows the day's decision not to seek 'the shadowy region' (Gondal?) but to turn to the inspiration of Nature—gray flocks, ferny glens, wild wind, mountains. And the final verse restates, in a new way once again, her most characteristic thought on nature, earth, heaven and the human spirit.

Index of First Lines